THE BAD SEX MANUAL

THE BAD SEX MANUAL

Peter Desberg, Ph.D. and
Tom McLoughlin Ph.D.less

Waterfront Press

Waterfront Press

copyright © 2016 Peter Desberg, Ph.D. and Tom McLoughlin Ph.D.less

Table of Contents

Part One: Male Problems
1. Premature Ejaculation ·6
2. Impotence · 27
3. Artful Refusal · 43
4A. Physical Attributes The Pot Belly · · · · · · · · · · · · · 59
4B. Physical Attributes The Small Organ · · · · · · · · · · · 73

Part Two: Female Problems
5. Frigidity · 88
6. Unstimulating · 106
7. Just Say "NO" · 120
8A. Physical Attributes: Underdeveloped · · · · · · · · · · 149
8B. Physical Attributes: Underdeveloped · · · · · · · · · · 149

Part Three: Gay Bad Sex
LGBT · 163

Part Four: Bad Sex in the Fast Lane
Bad Kinky Sex · 167

Part One: For Men

Introduction

Not a single one of the aspects of Bad Sex mentioned in this work has ever occurred in the lives of the authors. That does not mean, however, that the authors just made them up. We collected them using the most systematic data collection principles available to the scientific community. The authors were forced, methodologically speaking, to read books that appealed to the average reader's prurient interests, view X-rated films (in some cases XXX rated ones), peruse magazines sold in Adult-Only bookstores and interview many unsavory people. The authors have personally sacrificed so that their readers may reap the benefits of their scholarly pursuits.

Although the authors have not experienced Bad Sex first hand, they were surprised to discover the alarming frequency of its occurrence. Moreover, they were made aware that when it does occur, it causes a great deal of awkwardness and tension between the participants. Such consequences could easily lead to a deterioration of mental health throughout this great country of ours. So, at great personal expense, and an abiding concern for preserving and improving the psyche of the nation, the authors have set about solving this serious national crisis.

They present here, a series of verbal responses to the Bad Sex situation (or crisis if localized here in Southern California) that should aid the perpetrator of the Bad Sex response to rebound from the situation. And in the aggregate, we hope this will restore our country's potentially crumbling mental health structure.

Remember that the only way to stop bad sex from causing trauma is to have bad sex with a good response to avoid trauma.

A Note About The Photographs

Most people will quickly notice that the models are wearing clothes in situations where most people would not. There are two reasons that lead us to this decision:

1. Many of our readers have children. Readers will surely want to carry this book with them as much as possible. This may result in the book being left where young eyes might view it. We are concerned about protecting their young eyes and minds. If they want to see naked pictures, there are always National Geographic magazines to be viewed.
2. Our models refused to pose in the nude. Perhaps this explains why they are models for a book about Bad Sex.

What he can say when...
he did, but she didn't.
(It was over too quickly)

Chapter 1: Premature Ejaculation

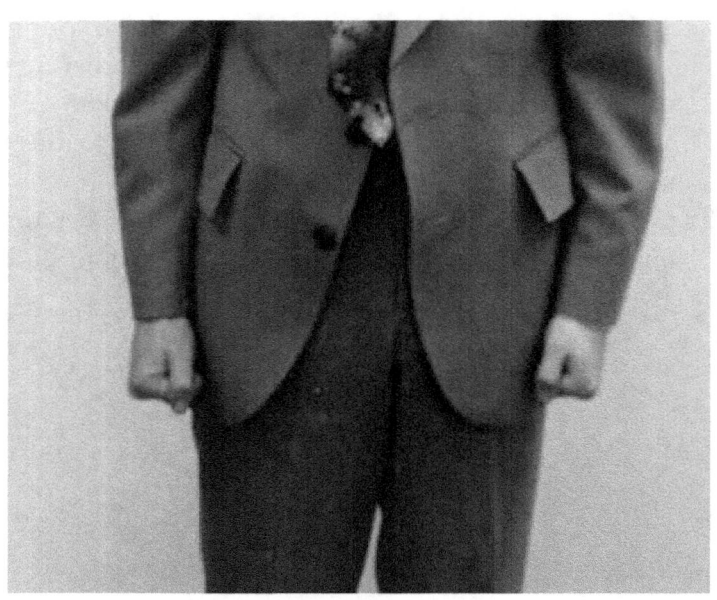

His Responses Explaining Away His Premature Ejaculation

- I told you I could put the condom on by myself, but oh no. You had to do it.

- When you arched your back, I thought you did, so I did.

- This never happens to me when I'm on the Internet.

- I'm so glad you're not the kind of woman who wants to make a man feel guilty.

- Why didn't you tell me you wanted to also?

- It's your fault. I wanted to skip the foreplay.

- Would it help to say I was sorry?

- I couldn't have done that if I didn't feel so comfortable with you.

- Maybe you did too, but you didn't notice. Check again.

- If we did this more often, I wouldn't get so excited.

Tension: A reliable indicator of Premature Ejaculation

Figure 1: Physical signs of Bad Sex – tension

- A woman as sensual as you must have this happen all the time.

- I shouldn't be doing this. I respect you way too much.

> ### Toolbox Tips to Control
> ### Premature Ejaculation – Relaxation
> An orgasm is a series of muscular contractions that release muscular tension. If you can learn to reduce tension by not contracting your muscles a lot, you can learn to control Premature Ejaculations. Breathing exercises are a good way to practice this. Begin your practice with situations that are less threatening. Here's an example. Begin a deep breathing exercise while you break up a dogfight between two large pit bulls. Then work your way up to the bedroom.

Sympathy Induction

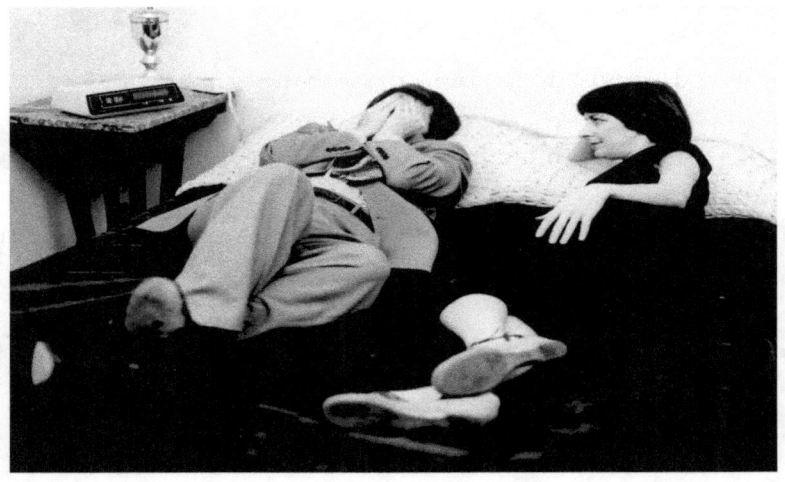

Figure 2: Post Bad Sex posture

- **CHECK ONE OF THE FOLLOWING:**

It's not my fault, I was raised:
    ___ a. Jewish
    ___ b. Roman Catholic
    ___ c. Baptist
    ___ d. In New Jersey

- Sorry, you just got me *so* excited!

- Usually, I can go for hours...no, seriously.

- Gee, it was like having my first sexual experience all over again.

- When I get too excited, I can get violent. I didn't want to hurt you.

- Why did you have to blow in my ear.

- It's not polite to laugh.

- Sexual compatibility is secondary, as long as the communication is there.

- All this mess came from me?

Little Known Bad Sex Facts: Plato was a premature ejaculator. This is not very surprising. All his students were male so he was rarely in the company of women. Worse still he and his students all wore skirts, resulting in serious gender identity issues.

Plato worked seven days a week and only had time to date on Ancient Greek holidays. Unlike the Hebrews who originally had two holidays per week, the ancient Greeks had only four holidays for the entire year. They didn't need more than that because of the vast array of sexual partners that Greek men had in those days.

Plato, unlike many other philosophers, didn't do part time work as a shepherd and was a committed heterosexual.

Percentage of Premature Ejaculations by Occupation

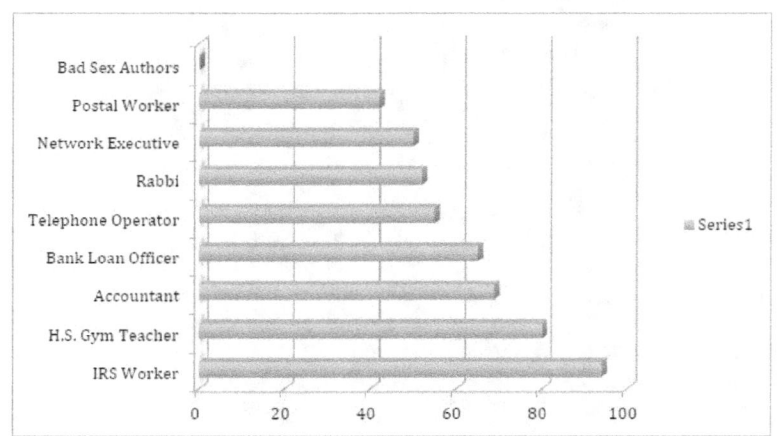

Table 1: Occupational Groups Representing the Highest Number of Premature Ejaculations

- CHECK ONE OF THE FOLLOWING:

It's my parents' fault for:
    ___ a. having me circumcised
    ___ b. not having me circumcised
    ___ c. laughing during my circumcision

Time Lapse photo of a man during Premature Ejaculation

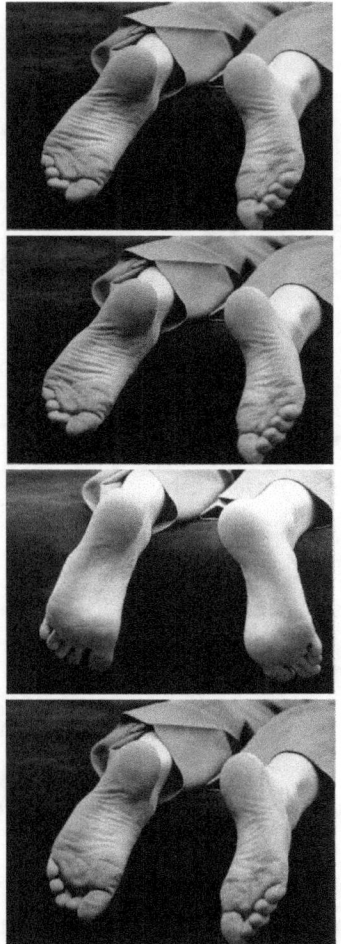

Figure 3: Time Lapse photographs of a man having a Premature Ejaculation

- I'm so sorry... but, it did feel fantastic.

- If it took me a long time, it would mean you didn't excite me anymore.

Women's Reactions to Premature Ejaculation

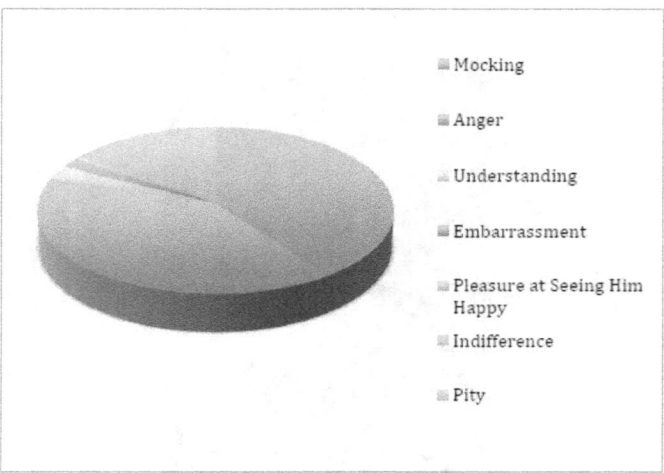

Table 2: Women's reactions, by percentage, to her partner's Premature Ejaculation

- You Bitch!!! Look what you did to me!

- Hey, I'm an Aries and you're a Sagittarius. Look it up.

- This is the second one tonight. The first one was when we danced.

- Owwww... cramp in my leg... had to stop... really hurts.

- I didn't realize that fasting would have this affect on me.

Locations of Premature Ejaculations by Frequency

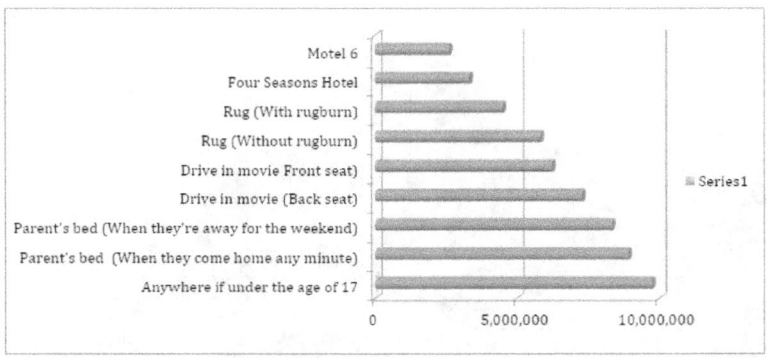

Table 3: Locations of Premature Ejaculations

- Just give me four or five more chances and it probably won't happen again.

- This only happened cause I truly like you.

- I was afraid I was too big and I was hurting you.

- You make me feel so young.

- I can't help it. I have a very high metabolism rate.

Blaming Your Partner

Figure 4: Blaming your partner

- I told you we should have waited a half hour after eating.

- We shouldn't have slow danced.

- I didn't want to spoil you for other men.

- Now let's see how good that vibrator of yours really is.

- The first three times each night are quick. But, the last two will seem like they last forever.

- I told you not to touch me *there*.

When she first discovers that he did, but she won't

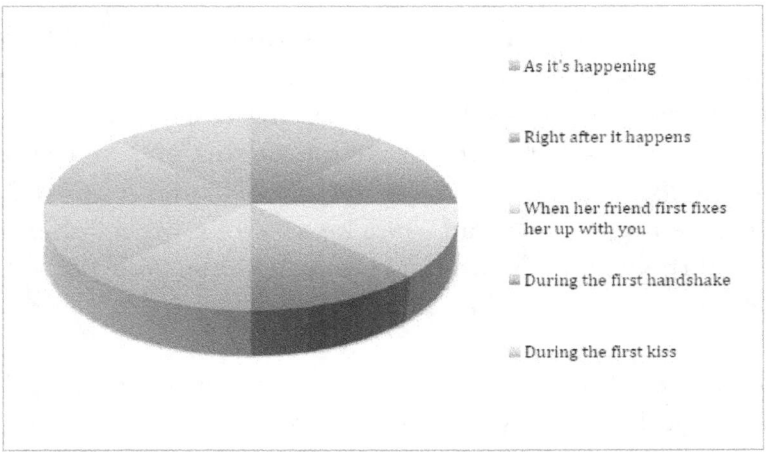

Table 4: When a woman first discovers that he did, but she won't.

- The next time can only get better.

- Maybe if you act more butch?

- I guess I'm not the best you've ever had.

- You shouldn't have screamed, "Oh God."

- Would it help to say, "I love you?"

- Would it help to say, "I *really* love you?"

- Masters and Johnson said we all must take responsibility for our own orgasms.

- For me, sex without emotional commitment just isn't satisfying. So call me old-fashioned.

Teaching Stories
Quick Mitch

When you first see Mitch, you probably say to yourself, "Not a bad looking guy." The female take is more like, "Hmmmm," but in the good sense. That was my first reaction at a bar on the Upper West Side. He bought me a drink and we chatted. He was 28, graduated from a good school, had a good job and presented well. I was glad when he asked for my number. He waited the necessary two days and called me. We went out to dinner.

The more I thought about him, the more I was surprised that he was still unattached and began wondering what might be wrong with him. There wasn't anything obvious that I could see. I relaxed and chalked it up to New York cynicism. We had dinner. It was a beautiful night so we walked around for a while. He kissed me goodnight at the door. So far, so good.

We went out again that Saturday night. He took me to a Knicks game. I love the Knicks, and to my surprise, so did he. A good sign. Then a late dinner. This time, I invited him in. To continue the mood, we had a few more beers and made out a little. Just as things started to get hot, he said he had to leave because he had to get up early in the morning. Early on Sunday morning? That's all he said and left.

We went out again on Friday night and this time, I invited him over for dinner. I lit a lot of candles; made sure I had a lot of his favorite wine, cooked a great dinner and then we settled in on the couch. We made out again and this time, I was a bit more aggressive and led him by the hand to the bedroom. We started to make love. As I was putting on the condom...boom. He ejaculated as I got it half way on. We had a few more awkward moments and he left...also quickly.

I didn't hear from Mitch for two weeks, so I called him. He seemed glad to hear from me and we decided to go out and see a movie. He planned the evening out meticulously so that we met at the movie theater, walked two blocks for dinner then said goodnight and we went home separately.

I was beginning to get an idea of why he was unattached, but he had so many good qualities that I had to give it another try. I invited him over again for dinner, and to not spook him, I told him it would be with two other couples. That seemed safe enough for him. What he didn't know was that I had arranged for both couples to leave right after dessert and we were alone again in my apartment. Soon we were alone in bed and this time got a little farther, but the key word here is *little*. Within twenty seconds of penetration his body convulsed and he began apologizing.

I tried to comfort him. He was reluctant to talk about it, but since we didn't have anything else to do, and he had quite a few glasses of wine, we talked. And we talked about everything except what I shall refer to as "the issue." I put on my robe and sat on the edge of the bed while he crawled under the covers pulling them up to his chin. I asked if he'd ever talked to any of his sexual partners about it. He said I was only his third partner and the other two didn't stick around long enough to talk. I told him I wasn't going anywhere.

Mitch said he was a shy kid with a terrible complexion until he was 22 years old. Until his face cleared up, he avoided any social interactions with girls except the ones *Esquire* magazine sent him every month, and of course, the *Sports Illustrated* Swimsuit edition. Later, he turned the job over to Hugh Heffner. Then he began relying on his new friend... the Internet. In talking to his college friends, he discovered that he was incredibly naïve about the opposite sex so now he added two new reasons to avoid girls: fear of embarrassment and ridicule.

By the time he was 23 he was surprised to discover that women actually found him attractive, but he felt like he was raised by wolves and had no idea of how to interact with them romantically. He tried a few clumsy dates that ended disastrously. But he found the courage to persist and got two women into bed. That's when he found a totally new appreciation for the depth of embarrassment and ridicule.

I thought, "Wow, this is like making it with a priest." I asked him if he would like to work through his issue. He said the feelings he had during his premature ejaculations was so intense, they could never be brought under control. I told him that if we made love every night for a week, he would begin to see a vast improvement. At the end of the week, I would say his improvement was half vast. So, I told him to call me in six months after he had some more mileage and we'll see how it goes. And I sorta' mean it.

- Don't confuse urgency with lack of control.

- I should never have looked down to see what was happening.

- How long do you usually stay angry?

- Why did you have to move?

- That was good and fast. Would you rather have long and boring?

- Now, that even surprised me.

- I really don't wanna' discuss it tonight. In the morning we'll both be more clear-headed.

- Why are you upset, isn't the purpose of sex to have an orgasm?

- Can I at least help you clean up?

- That was just lubricant…wait.

- Well, good night…

> **The Bad Sex Manual Hall of Fame**
> - Honest, this has *never* happened to me before.
> - You're just too hot.
> - OOOooops!!!
> - More than three minutes of foreplay and see what happens?

> ### Toolbox Tips to Control Premature Ejaculation – The *Start and Stop* Method
>
> The first step in this method is to discover when your point of "ejaculatory inevitability," or your "point-of-no-return" is reached. This is the moment just before you are about to explode. Then, instead of ejaculating, stop all forms of stimulation and allow the feelings to diminish. After you have regained control, start again. This exercise should be practiced alone at first.
>
> We suggest starting with a milder form of the exercise. Allow yourself to get very hungry (maybe 10 hours of food deprivation), walk up to a succulent buffet and indulge in the look and smell of each item, then abstain from eating for the next two days.

After this, try going to strip clubs. If you feel like the signs of "inevitability" are starting, run out to the parking lot without putting on your jacket. You may return and repeat until you gain more self-control.

After completing the Strip Club Stage, you are now ready to begin dating and having sex. You will now discover that your newly acquired powers of self-control with your date are incredibly strong... unless you make the mistake of letting her touch you.

Confuse Your Partner by Acting Smug

Figure 5. Post Bed Posture – Smugness

Peter Desberg, Ph.D. and Tom McLoughlin Ph.D.less

Time Lapse photo of both man and woman during Premature Ejaculation

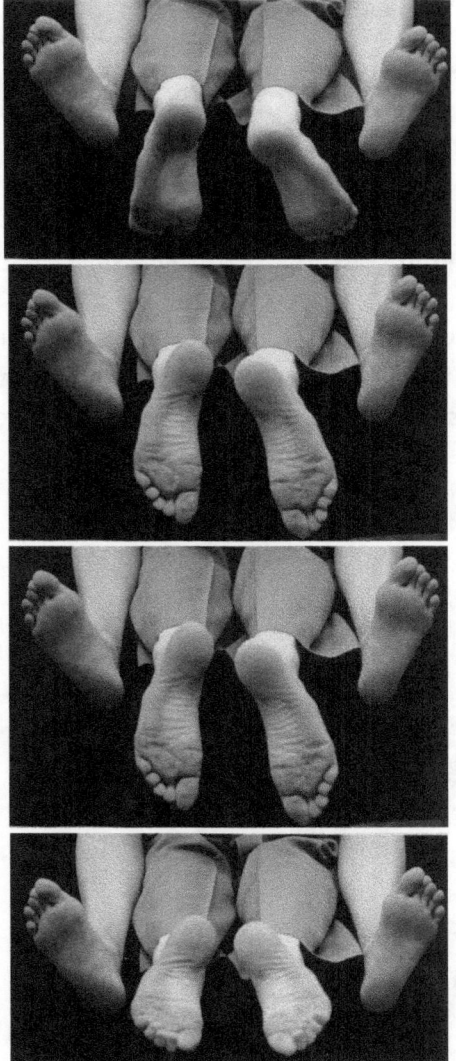

Figure 6. Both Partners' feet during Premature Ejaculation

Clinical Recommendations: Premature Ejaculation
1. Begin pleasuring yourself 3 times a day two weeks prior to your date.
2. Create source material for distracting thoughts (e.g., images of baseball players or tugboats) a week before so you won't fold under pressure and come up empty.
3. Identify the most painful place where you can pinch yourself if you begin to feel early signs of "you know what."
4. On the date, avoid any unnecessary touching until you are both undressed and in bed.
5. When you begin having intercourse, try to think of any sermon you have ever heard given to teens in any house of worship. The more guilt and shame you can dredge up, the better.
6. Once you begin doing it... good luck. You're on your own.

Thing To Avoid for Premature Ejaculators
1. Touching women
2. Any sexual thoughts
3. Oysters
4. Pornography
5. Going outside

The Case of Marty M.

There were three significant events in Marty's pre 18 year-old life. The first was when he was 15. He was sitting in his history class next to Barbara. He had lots of dreams about Barbara, but knew he never had a chance with her. One day, as he was missing most of the lecture and squirming in his seat so Barbara wouldn't notice his erection, she dropped her pencil. As she reached for it, she accidently brushed him... down there. It was very brief, but he felt something like a volcano erupting in his pants. He swooned a little, then looked down and found that his pants were wet and sticky. He didn't know what to make of it, and spent the rest of the class praying his pants would dry soon.

A year later, he was in the lunch line and some guys were shoving each other. Then, one of the guys bumped into Marty. He lurched forward, just as Gina Cartucci was bending over to pick up the napkin she'd dropped. That was the second time. The third time was at a party making out with an overweight girl that he barely knew, but she was willing to make out and he once again left with moist trousers.

Marty is now 27 years old. He has had sex with three partners and on each of the five occasions; he has had very premature ejaculations. The first two occurred while his partner was putting on his condom. The third was while he was putting it on by himself. By numbers four and five, he achieved penetration, but not for long.

Treatment 1: The therapist tried to get Marty to concentrate on something non-sexual while engaging in coitus. He suggested basketball. Marty tried this. He worked very hard only to discover that it didn't help his problem, and now, as soon as a basketball game starts on TV, he starts breathing heavily.

Treatment 2: The therapist's next suggestion was a pre-ejaculation strategy. He suggested that Marty engage in masturbatory activity prior to his dates. Dutifully, Marty tried this autoerotic activity in the afternoon; then went on his date. It was unsuccessful. He still ejaculated prematurely. So the therapist suggested that he try to double his masturbatory output before his next date. Marty did this. Then when the moment of truth arrived, between the fear of premature ejaculation he felt, and the prior depletion exercise, Marty was unable to maintain an erection (He is now reading the next chapter of this book).

Treatment 3: Marty has joined the Premarital Abstinence Club at his church and doesn't worry any more. But at the meetings, he has to be very careful whom he bumps into.

What he can say when...
he can't get it up.
(The hard truth about Impotence.)

Chapter 2: Impotence

His Responses To Explain His Impotence

- Maybe if you'd stop staring at it.

- It's a little difficult for me with your father's picture hanging over the bed.

- I could... if I really wanted to.

- Who are you texting?

- I told you I shouldn't have had that second glass of wine.

- You shouldn't have snuck up and grabbed it like that.

- I guess I respect you too much.

- I think it has something to do with the full moon.

- Quick... talk dirty to me.

- Damn documentary... all those orphans in Africa.

- Your beauty intimidates me.

- I think it's because you're Catholic.

The Limp Look: A Sure Indicator of Impotence

Figure 1: Physical Indicators of Impotence – The Limp Look

- It's because your hands are too cold.

- Your perfume reminds me of my mother.

- I wish you hadn't told me how you've been looking forward to this all week.

- If God had wanted me to have an erection, he would have given you larger breasts.

- My therapist says the man and woman both have to share in the responsibility.

- **CHOOSE ONE OF THE FOLLOWING:**

It's too _____ in here.

    ___ a. hot
    ___ b. cold
    ___ c. stuffy
    ___ d. dirty
    ___ e. bright
    ___ f. dark
    ___ g. perfect

Toolbox Tips to Control Impotence – The Little Blue Pill

We've all heard of Viagra. And we know that it, and related pills work...sort of. But, take a quick look at the most common side-effects of Viagra. They include headaches, stomach pain, nasal congestion, nausea, diarrhea, and an inability to differentiate between the colors green and blue, loss of hearing, ringing in the ears and dizziness, numbness, or tingling in your chest, arms, neck, or jaw, dyspepsia, rash, chills, shock, chest pain, migraine, tachycardia, heart failure, vomiting rectal hemorrhaging and gingivitis. We'd go on except that we do have some space limitations, whereas, the number of side effects of Viagra don't seem to be burdened with such limitations.

- This happened after the accident. I don't want to talk about it.

- This only happens when I'm in love.

- Wait a minute. Are you putting this into a spreadsheet?

- You had to say I was "short and ugly?"

Who Women Blame for a Man's Impotence

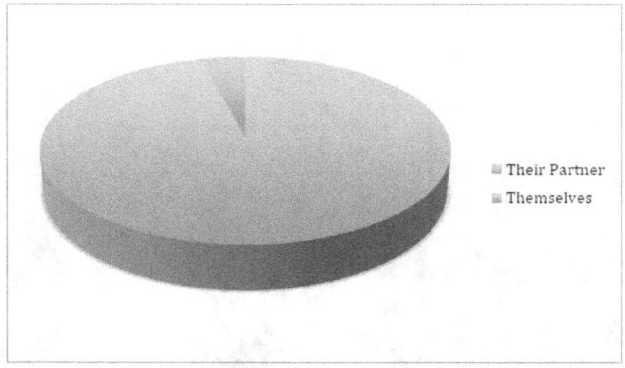

Table 1: Percentage of blame women place with impotence

- Maybe if you put on this garter belt.

- Black/White, Yin/Yang, hard/soft... they're just polarities. Cosmically, they're the same thing.

> ### Toolbox Tips to Control Impotence – Lifestyle Changes
>
> Medical science has shown us that through a few simple alterations in our lifestyle we can go a long way toward dealing with erectile dysfunction (the politically correct way to say "Impotence"). Here are a few of the more prominent changes that should help you. You can begin a vigorous exercise program such as running a few miles a day or joining a Mixed Martial Arts Training gym. Going on a severe diet and losing 30 – 50 pounds has also been shown to help. If you smoke... stop immediately. Seriously reduce your alcohol consumption limiting yourself to two glasses of beer a week. This plan will surely work because you will get into such a bad mood that no woman will want to be anywhere near you, so... no more impotence worries.

Averting Anger Through Cuteness

Figure 2: Impotence Posture 2 – Cuteness

- Try saying, "Wake up the little giant?"

- Couldn't we just talk tonight.

- Shouldn't have gone to Bible Study.

- You're already making demands on the relationship?

- I tried to tell you that I was ticklish.

Teaching Stories
Up, Up and Away

Jan was sorta' cute, at least she thought she was on her good days. On her bad days, she needed proof. She'd go to bars and see how many guys would offer to buy her drinks. She kept track of the number on her iPhone. She'd go to museums because she read that guys have fantasies about meeting the perfect girl at a museum. It sounded right, after all she read it in Cosmo. She got a small dog so she could walk it around town and see how many guys stopped to pet it so they had an excuse to talk to her. This is just a small sample of her testing.

When she was in one of her many short-lived relationships, she used sex as an indicator. How soon would he try for a first kiss? How long did it take until he made the "big move?" How strong was his erection? How many times a night did he... could he?

She probably could have enjoyed sex if she hadn't been consumed with gathering statistics during it. But it didn't matter because it all changed during her first night under the sheets with Everett. Everything went smoothly until the first time they were both undressed under the sheets and she reached over and the words that jumped into her brain were, "Overcooked pasta."

Since it was dark, she thought maybe Everett had to see more of her so she lit a few candles. She wanted light, but didn't want to break the mood. Nothing. She tried lips, mouth, derriere and still no change. She tried to tell herself that there was something wrong with him, but all she could come back to was that she was failing "The Test." She wasn't cute enough and she wasn't sexy enough.

She slinked out of bed, quickly put on a robe and suggested that they have a glass of wine. Everett was fine with that. The wine got them feeling pretty loose and they talked late into the night. But while Jan might have looked very calm, her head was spinning. She kept changing poses trying to look sexier. She'd subtly find ways to brush up against the pasta and furtively look for any signs of stirring. Nothing.

Eventually, the lateness of the hour and the smoothness of the wine had their way. She fell asleep in Everett's arms and that's how they found themselves when they awoke and each tried to hide their stale breath from the other. They each had to go to work so they were spared any further awkwardness. Jan liked everything about Everett except for... So we was very happy when Everett asked her out for dinner on Saturday night. She didn't bother acting coy. She accepted and immediately started making plans to avoid having a repetition of the previous night.

She went out and bought a very provocative new dress, got a hair appointment, found a very small bottle of expensive perfume knowing she had to go without lunch for a few days to afford it. She asked friends for music recommendations, asked other friends for any seductive advice they had to offer. Then she called Everett and said she would like to cook dinner for him. She asked her promiscuous friend Zoe for a list of the most potent foods that were likely to stimulate a man's other appetite. Everything was ready for the big night.

As Everett as showered, he looked down, cleared his throat and addressed his genitals. "Please, just this one night... work! You don't have any trouble when we watch porn on the Internet together, why won't you work with a real girl?" He didn't wait for an answer.

When Everett consulted a shrink, he heard the same advice that the two previous shrinks gave him. "Just relax and enjoy it." But they didn't understand his problem. Perhaps it was because he never told them about it. Had he told them, it would have gone like this.

When Everett was fifteen years old, his sister Eileen, who was almost seventeen burst into his room one night giggling. She had been drinking beer at a party and seemed pretty tipsy. Elaine was very pretty and knew it. She liked to sit in boys' laps and wiggle around until she could feel their erections and then jump right onto the next lap. She loved to tease. Everett would try to peek into her room when she was changing or showering and Elaine knew it and enjoyed torturing Everett. Everett was the opposite of Elaine. He never had a date, never went to parties and never got near any of the girls he fantasized about. His lap was always empty.

Elaine burst into Everett's room that night to find Everett's pajama pants down and he had a ménage a trois going on. Everett and the two centerfolds his magazines were open to. Elaine jumped up on the bed and pulled on the blanket that Everett frantically tried to cover himself with. Everett tugged while Elaine laughed. Then she said, "Have you ever had it touched by a girl?" She drank a lot of beers that night. Long story short, she convinced Everett to let her see him and just stroke it a few times. It was not a difficult sale. As soon as she touched him... boom. Everett had a cascading premature ejaculation.

Elaine pulled her hand back in horror. She sobered up very quickly and began cursing at Everett and calling him a sick pervert. It was surreal for Everett. As she was running into the bathroom to clean her hand, she was screaming, but in a low voice so she wouldn't wake up their parents. For weeks, Everett avoided eye contact, which was easy because Elaine put as much distance between them as the house would allow. Everett felt very, very dirty.

Jan and Everett tried to have sex a few more times with the same result. This went on for three and a half months. Most couples would have talked about it. Everett avoided talking about it, but knew it was his fault and it was just way too painful to talk about. Jan, on the other hand avoided talking about it because she knew it was her fault. She wasn't alluring enough.

One day, Jan was having lunch with a friend and let it slip out. Her friend said she went out with several guys who had trouble "getting it up." Armed with the powerful knowledge that, just maybe, it wasn't totally her fault, she asked Everett if they could talk about it. Everett calmly got dressed, left Jan's apartment and they never saw each other again.

- Thanks for understanding. You're very empathic.

- You can't fight gravity.

- Would you take it wrong if I asked you to brush your teeth?

- At least we can be sure that I didn't get you pregnant.

- While we're just waiting, have you heard any good gossip lately?

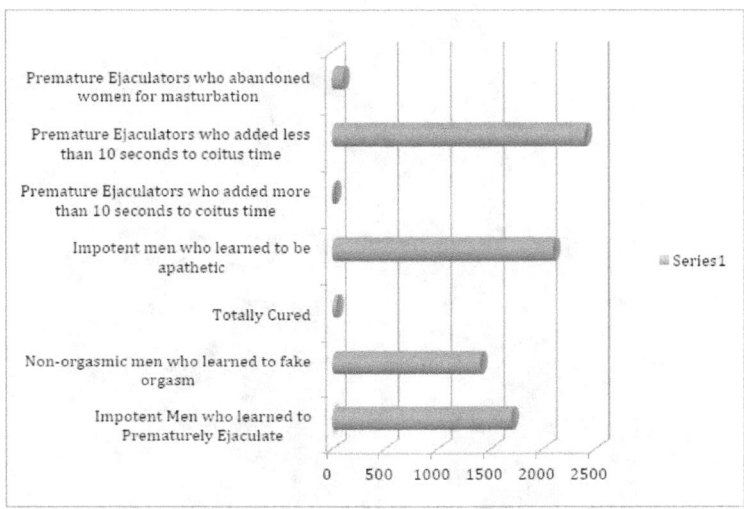

Table 2: Number of men who have been helped by a Sex Therapist

- Maybe if you stopped laughing.

- It might also help if you stopped pointing and laughing.

- I'm working on not being controlled by my basic drives.

- The vinyl in the back seat's too cold.

Little Known Bad Sex Facts: Thomas Edison is not smiling in this picture because he had a sexual life plagued with impotence. He had few problems until he invented the light bulb and could no longer have sex in the dark with his wife. He went on to invent the phonograph so he could play romantic music during sex, but it didn't do the trick. It is a well-known fact that he also invented the motion picture camera, but few people were privy as to why he invented it. He had a dream to create pornography. Sadly he did not live long enough to see it. He had a large collection of French nude postcards, but shaking them vigorously did not really make them animate.

- You only agreed to it because you knew this would happen.

- Maybe if you stopped eyeing your vibrator.

- Is that all you think about?

- Just give it 18 more minutes.

- I took you to dinner and a show, what more do you want?

Becoming a Mysterious Stranger

Figure 3: Impotence Posture 3 – Mysterious Stranger

- Could you try rubbing my back instead?

- I'm afraid if I do it this time, you'll always expect it.

- This is just like my Driving Test all over again.

Pretend You Are Asleep

Figure 4: Pretending That You Are Asleep

- CHOOSE ONE OF THE FOLLOWING:

Would you mind removing your _____?
    ___ a. Crucifix
    ___ b. Star of David
    ___ c. Your "What Would Jesus Do" bracelet

Toolbox Tips to Control Impotence – Acupuncture

Medical research has shown that acupuncture can been effective in about 20–30% of the cases where it has been tried. Apparently, the biggest problem is where the acupuncturist is located during foreplay.

- Maybe if you hadn't beaten me in tennis?

- Perhaps if you took off your rubber gloves?

- Maybe if you got dressed, and then slowly undressed again.

> **The Bad Sex Manual Hall of Fame**
> - This has never happened to me before.
> - I guess my feelings for you run deeper than I thought.
> - This is all your fault!

Clinical Recommendations: Impotence
1. Eat Oysters
2. Think lewd thoughts
3. (Repeat if necessary)

Thing To Avoid for Men With Impotence
1. Aggressive women
2. Male Underwear ads
3. Soft Frozen Yogurt
4. Large women
5. Butch women

> **The Case of Franco C.**
> On a Sunday afternoon, at the age of 14, Franco inadvertently walked into his parents' bedroom and caught his hairy, overweight mother and smooth skinny father engaged in coitus. Frozen in a mixture of fear and fascination, he watched for what he thought was a very long time, which turned out to be 14 seconds.

Since that time, the sight of the naked female form has produced a mixture of emotions that he describes as, "An erotic, shameful, resplendent abomination." These conflicting thoughts leave him impotently unaroused.

Treatment 1: The therapist suggested that he discreetly view pornographic videos on the computer. This would help desensitize him to the sex act. He insisted that the females should always be young, thin and definitely hairless. Instead of curing his impotence, Franco now has added guilt and shame to his growing list of problems. To date, his problems are the only thing growing.

Treatment 2: The therapist began creating a set of guided imagery sessions for Franco. He was told to picture his mother as an angel, and his father a saint. Then, in an effort to further the discrimination, he told Franco to picture his sexual partners as streetwalkers and call girls. Franco has been arrested twice for solicitation. He revealed that on three occasions he purchased the use of what he referred to as "sex surrogates who worked curbside." In court it was quickly revealed that they were prostitutes. He pointed out that in each case, as they tried to help him become aroused, he called them, "Mother."

Franco C. is currently coaching 9 year-old girls in an AYSO soccer league. He still cannot get an erection when attempting coitus, but believes he is making progress because he has never called any of the young girls "Mother."

What he can say when…
she wants to, but he doesn't.
(Turning it down.)

Chapter 3: Artful Refusals

Responses for Refusing

- It'll make me want you more tomorrow.

- You'd think the way I wanted to do it was too dirty.

- I enjoy being with you, just not physically.

What part of, "No, I don't want to give in to my baser instincts while I accept the notion that we were put here on Earth to serve a higher purpose and I am committed to moving the world toward harmony with every fiber in my body," don't you understand?

- I got a blister from last night.

- If my mother would find out, it would kill her.

- Sorry, I just ate.

- You're just waiting for me to agree so you can change your mind.

Note: The following Figures (1 – 5) are photographs illustrating the five basic facial expressions that indicate, with certainty, that a man is lying when declining a sexual invitation.

Lying About Refusing – Smiling

Figure 1: Lying about refusing – Smiling

- I can't chance it. Tomorrow they're checking my prostate.

- I just read my first romance novel. I'm not willing to make love that lasts seven pages.

- If your brother found out, he'd kill me.

- It's been a while and it would be over way too quickly.

- I'm afraid if we do, you'll become too attached.

- Nice girls don't talk this way.

Teaching Stories
The Responsibility of "No"

Gina loved working in Silicon Valley. Why shouldn't she? She was 22 years old, moderately attractive and didn't hide it. Because it was a high tech social media marketing group, they were too cool to have offices, or even cubicles, except for the CEO who had his office on a loft on the upper level of the building. That meant whenever she got up to walk around, there were many eyes following her. That was one of the perks of working there.

She loved working around the mental power that permeated this massive room. Even more, she loved the fact that most of the employees were nerdy men. They were brilliant, and massively cowed by pretty girls. Every day as she walked in she'd think, "Let the stammering begin." The other women who worked there looked pretty much like the men except they had smaller feet.

Gina worked in the Graphic Arts Podule (a name they came up with by combining the words "pod" and "module.") She worked right in the middle of the entire space so even if she wasn't walking around, almost ever man, and a few women, found a reason to come see her or at least walk by on their way to somewhere else.

As Gina got up every morning, looked in her closet and let out a breathy sigh, she said to herself, "How do I want to titillate them today?" The company had a policy that employee dating was frowned upon. But because they were out-of-the-box, lateral thinking intellectual rebels, they were proud that nobody cared about following conventional policy. Gina received offers daily and even took a few of them. But she just looked at work as a place to flirt and watch men clumsily paw at her with their intellects. All of them except for James.

James
To get it off the table right away, James is not gay. He's focused. He likes the work he does. He's consumed by it. Of course he notices Gina, but doesn't seem to be entranced by her the way his co-workers are. A lot of the time when she walks by, James is so fixated on his project he doesn't even notice. But Gina does. Getting James became Gina's mission.

James was heading a big social media incursion into the area of free-range farming. Once Gina found out, she searched Google so she'd have a daily nutrition question for him. One day at lunchtime, she went to a vegan restaurant and got two sandwiches to go. Although she didn't make a serious dent in hers, James consumed his with vigor. This, together with her frequent walk-bys with charming smiles did not go unnoticed. Except by James. It made total sense to him that Gina wanted to learn more about healthy living and nutrition. He was glad to help.

Then fortune struck. There was a big Free Range Farming conference down in Los Angeles and the company asked James to represent them. They would make all the arrangements. When he got on the plane, he was surprised to find Gina in the seat next to him. "They wanted some video footage of the conference so they sent me with you." Gina had to cash in some favors and do a bit of politicking, but there she was sitting next to James. She still wasn't sure she really liked him at all, but it became essential for her to find out if she could *get* him.

The first night of the conference had a dinner speaker, some wonderfully fresh food and an ending time of 7:15 PM. What do you expect from a bunch of farmers? Gina giggled and said, "Look what someone gave me today." She pulled out a bottle of organic wine bottled in a small vineyard in a corner of a large organic farm. "The sweet farmer who gave it to me was very proud of it and made me promise to let him know what I thought of it. Would you like to sample it with me James?"

James was a little flustered, but it was really early. It would be more awkward to refuse than to accept, so he did. Gina apologized about only having a bed to sit on in her hotel room and began pouring. By the end of the third, or was it the fourth glass of wine, James was feeling warm and mellow. Gina was careful to avoid getting too close, too early. Now seemed like the right time.

Soon they were kissing and fondling. She took off her blouse, and even in the dim light, he noticed that she wasn't wearing a bra. She helped him out of his shirt. The two of them were giggling, grinding and pawing at each other, but as soon as things moved seriously below the waist, James sat bolt upright and said, "No, this is wrong. I can't do this." He jumped out of bed and began getting dressed.

A stunned Gina pulled on her blouse and said, "I'm not used to men saying 'No' to me. Especially when things have gone this far. Don't you think you at least owe me an explanation?"

James said. "There's something you don't know about me. It's difficult to talk about. But because the wine had warmed him up, he asked if she wanted to hear his story. She nodded her head.

James' Story
About a year-and-a-half ago, I was sitting at home alone. The phone rang and a woman said she wanted to talk to me for a moment, but said it was a little embarrassing for her. She said she was having lunch with a friend about a month ago. After a few glasses of wine, this friend told her about having the most

incredible sexual experience of her life. Then she mentioned that it was with you.

She said, "I wrote off the story as a side effect of the wine. Then, at dinner three weeks ago, I had dinner with another friend and heard almost the same story. Two hours ago, it happened again, with a different girlfriend. And frankly, and here's the awkward part of the story, I'd like to get together with you."

James asked her to tell him who put her up to playing this trick on him. She said it was no trick. Then she named her three friends. He realized that he had been out with all three of them around the times she said. Her story seemed true. "Then, she told me some of the things they said I did to them. Before he could respond, she asked if he was free at the moment. She would like to come over…right away. Within twenty minutes she was knocking at the door. Five minutes after that, we were undressed and in bed. And after five minutes of intercourse, she jumped out of bed grabbed her clothes and began screaming at me."

"You need to be more careful. You don't seem to understand the power you have over women. I'm leaving before you ruin sex with other men for me. You should be more responsible. It's like you don't understand what you have." And with that, she slammed the door.

Hearing this story got Gina very aroused. As she made a playful grab for his crotch, he looked very forlorn and said, "I'm sorry, but I do have to exercise some responsibility. I can't have what would happen to you on my conscience. I have to leave now."

Jeffrey
Jeffrey was James' best friend. A year-and-a-half ago, he couldn't figure out what to get James for his 30th birthday. He brought up this issue in his weekly group therapy session. Marlene said

she had a suggestion. She was an out-of-work makeup artist who owned up to being a nymphomaniac. But that wasn't the problem she joined the group to work on. She possessed a wicked sense of humor and presented Jeffrey with an idea. Marlene got Jeffrey to give her the names of the three girls he knew James had gone out with. He also told her about some of the sexual techniques that he tried in a freaky sex book they had both read. Marlene did the rest.

Jeffrey wanted to tell James about the joke, but didn't have the heart to take the experience away from James. And James was just looking for the right girl to settle down with and ruin for all other men. Gina is still prowling around at work and is obsessed with finding new vegan restaurants so she can share lunch with James... and maybe more.

- Do you realize that God is watching us right now?

- I wish I didn't know your family so well.

- I've got my reputation to think about.

- You believe that's all guys think about... don't you?

- I live at home and my mom checks my underwear carefully when she does the laundry.

- Your short hair threatens my masculinity.

- I just don't think of you *that* way.

Lying About Refusing – Sad

Figure 2: Lying about refusing – Sad

- I'm not just a hunk of meat.
- I'm not as good as I look.

Rejected Sexual Partner by Occupation

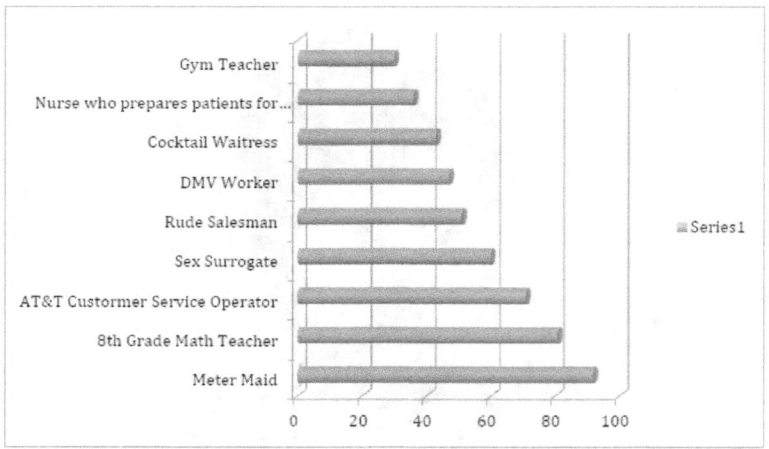

Table 1: Probability of being rejected by sexual partner (by occupation)

- I didn't shower today. I'd be too self-conscious.

- I heard you weren't that good.

> ### Toolbox Tips to Control Guilt over Refusing
> Some psychologists say that guilt is a manipulative way of looking for forgiveness. They think that if you suffer because you said "No," she might forgive you. Since only you can forgive yourself... forget about it and move on.

- Doesn't anybody just talk anymore?

Little Known Bad Sex Facts: Even most biblical scholars don't know that Goliath had a sexual dysfunction. He couldn't say "no" to any woman who wanted to have sex with him. Those same scholars misinterpreted his fight with David. They believe David won because Goliath represented Evil and David represented Good. NO! Goliath was just too tired from having so much sex with five women the night before the big fight.

- I don't perform on command.

- Can I be honest? I just like you for your mind?

- Hey... my eyes are up here.

- Wow, are you oversexed.

- You know that it hurts me to say, "No" to you.

- I'm intimidated by aggressive women.

- If you tell everyone how good I am, it'll end up going viral.

Lying About Refusing – Seductive

Figure 3: Lying about refusing – Seductive

- What if we start and I don't arouse you enough?

- I won't let my glands run my life.

- You're not enough of a challenge for me.

- Let's get something to eat and then discuss it.

- If I didn't say, "No" you'd think I was weak.

Lying About Refusing – Angry

Figure 4: Lying about refusing – Angry

- Just because I bought you dinner doesn't mean that I have to go to bed with you.

- My sisters would kill you if they found out.

- You may have heard about my reputation, but I'm not that easy.

Lying About Refusing – Passive

Figure 5: Lying about refusing – Passive

- I can't take the chance. This could ruin everything we've worked so hard to achieve in our relationship.

- "Do this...do that!" You sound like my mother.

The Bad Sex Manual Hall of Fame
- I'm not in the mood.
- Sorry, I have to get up early in the morning.
- I'm wearing dirty underwear.

Clinical Recommendations: The Art Of Refusal
1. Feign illness
2. Be descriptive about each symptom
3. Talk about being contagious

Thing To Avoid for Men Refusing Sex
1. Aggressive women
2. Passive women
3. Women

The Case of Benny G.

Benny grew up in a house with pervasive negativity. He didn't bother to ask for anything because he knew the answer would be "No." From an early age, he vowed to be positive all the time. He tried to grant any request; even if it came from someone he didn't like. Being so affable proved to be helpful in the business world and he soon found himself working as an assistant to the head of a big movie studio. He became a legendary "Yes Man." In his spare time, he belonged to an improv troupe. He was lured into improv when he heard that the most important skill was to always say, "Yes" to whatever suggestion came his way. Everything in his life was going well until he began dating.

Between being likable and working for the head of a studio, women threw themselves at him. At first, he tried to accommodate them all, but soon found that he just wasn't up to the task. But how could he learn to say "No" without making them feel bad?

Treatment 1: His therapist suggested that he begin saying "No" gradually. If a woman asked if he was thirsty, he should just say "No."

(Yes...you guessed it. Benny had a problem with the War on Drugs. He couldn't just say "No.") His first attempt was close. When she asked if he was thirsty, he said, "No ... well maybe just a little." At this point he still can't refuse sex, but he has become quite dehydrated. His therapist looks at this as a small triumph.

Treatment 2: His therapist then suggested that he learn to negotiate with women. He suggested that if a woman wants sex, he should say OK, if she washed his clothes. At this time, he is still having sex whenever asked, but there is not a dirty pair of underwear or socks to be found in his apartment.

What he can say when...
she sees his pot belly.
(A big problem)

Chapter 4A:
Physical Attributes
The Pot Belly

Responses for explaining away his pot belly

- I've been too busy making money to exercise.

- My gym membership ran out last week.

- You'll be having sex with my essence, not my body.

The Pot Belly – Before Camouflage

Figure 1: Pre-camouflaged Pot Belly

- It swells up like this when I'm aroused.

- I'm going to give up desserts...just for you.

- Anyone who wants to can buy one of those weightlifter bodies.

- I still look great from the back.

- It's all from Chinese food. In half an hour, it'll be flat again.

The Pot Belly – Attaché Case Camouflage

Figure 2: The Attaché Case Camouflage

Foods to Avoid

Nestle's Quick	Minute Steak
Crushed Nuts	Soft Frozen Yogurt
Jiffy Pop	Chili or Beans
Shrimp	Instant Lunch
Meat Loaf	Quick Creamed Zucchini
Popovers	Frozen Tuna Casserole
Minute Maid	Snickers
Sort Ribs	Adolph's Meat Tenderizer

Table 1: Foods to avoid

Foods to Increase

Wild Rice
Hamburger Helper
Carefree Gum
7 Up
Hot Dog Relish
Puffed Rice
Betty Crocker Super Moist Cake Mix

Table 2: Foods to Increase

Foods for the Adventurous

Pop-up Tarts
Cool Whip
Gooseberries
French Cheesecake
Honeybuns
Large cucumbers and zucchinis
Dream Whip

Table 3: Adventurous food

- My soul has a six-pack.

Little Known Bad Sex Facts: Napoleon was always pictured with his hand tucked into his jacket. Some people said it was for warmth, some said it was for style, but historians have finally revealed the actual reason. Napoleon always over ate. He had a huge gut and if it wasn't for an elaborate set of corsets that he was laced into every morning by a staff of six, the whole world would have known about it. His hand tuck was a little insurance that the corsets were working.

Any artist who depicted him accurately was immediately beheaded. Have you ever wondered why we don't have any actual photographs of Napoleon? The cause of his weight problem originated with the pastry that bore his name. He was so proud of it that it was all he ever ate. He had the second worst diet in history, following only by the King...Elvis.

- You know, the quickest way to a man's heart really isn't his stomach.

- Eating is a form of sensuality and I'm enormously sensual.

- You can rub it for luck.

- You can rest your head on it when we're watching TV.

- The size of a man's stomach indicates the size of his sexual appetite.

The Pot Belly – Crossed Arms Camouflage

Figure 3: The Crossed Arms Camouflage

- It's all from health foods.

- I'm told it makes me look distinguished.

Teaching Stories

Pot Luck

Andrew and Allison got married seven years ago and no one was surprised. They met in Law School and discovered they had a lot in common. They liked the same restaurants, the same films even the same basketball team. Their relationship didn't begin with a scorching infatuation. They just seemed to be together a lot and decided they might as well go out. They were too wrapped up in their studies to go out to bars or parties to meet other people so the two of them just found it convenient to pair up.

All during their clerkship and bar preparation they found it nice to have someone to study and commiserate with. When they both got jobs with large law firms, it just seemed sensible to marry. Not much as love stories go.

Allison got up at 5:00 A.M. every morning to run for an hour. She said it cleared her head and kept her energy level up. She also liked the way she looked in the mirror. Andrew used to join her. Occasionally, when he was up late at night working, he begged off. As time went on, he jogged a bit less and jiggled a bit more.

One night, after completing a case that he worked on for long hours over many months, he came home, casually walked into the bathroom, took off his shirt and got the shock of his life.

He had a grown a potbelly. No! He had always been in such good shape. Well, kinda' good shape. How could this have happened? That was an easy one. Andrew was working so hard that he lost track of all the late night dinners, drinking with staff and clients and the fact that he couldn't remember the last time he went running with Allison.

Their schedules had become so separate that they hardly saw each other. They were going to celebrate his finishing this big case by going to Aruba for a long weekend. He panicked. "I can't let her see me like this." He got down on the floor and started doing sit-ups as fast as he could. In his panicked state, he started picturing the two of them on the beach, Allison in her skimpy bikini and he in his tight European bathing suit. He began to shake uncontrollably.

As he tried to calm himself down, he started thinking about all the subtle cues he had been ignoring lately. His suit trousers weren't closing easily, which he wrote off as styles were becoming tighter. So he went out and bought new ones. How could this have happened so fast? More importantly, Allison would be home in a few hours so they could start packing for the trip.

He ran down to the mall and got loaded. He bought several oversized Hawaiian shirts that camouflaged his midsection nicely. He even bought Allison one so he wouldn't arouse her suspicion. It was cute. They could dress like a married couple…the kind they used to make fun of. Next, he bought some very baggy shorts and very baggy drawstring pants. His panic began to fade a little. He went home to a euphoric wife who was very happy to be going away with him.

She said, "You know, we don't have to start packing right away. We've been missing each other just about every day. It's been a long time since we snuggled."

Andrew panicked. "Snuggled" was their code word to initiate sex. It was four in the afternoon. Very light outside and worse, inside. Andrew said, "If this is really a holiday, we don't have to wait for Aruba. Let's start right now. Grab your coat, I'm taking you out for a romantic dinner to start things off."

As Allison protested, Andrew wouldn't hear of it. If they were going to, they would do it right. It got dark around 7:00 so if they got cleaned up and dressed he could hold her off until dark. He carefully choreographed their cleaning and dressing routines so that they weren't in the same location together. He put on a loose fitting sweater and carried a jacket to conceal any view of his newly acquired real estate.

They got home at dusk, Andrew insisted on lighting a small candle as a romantic touch. She thought it was cute and he bumped his shin on the nightstand. He switched off the light and said, "Come darling." The next morning, he made it a point to get up way earlier than Allison. He put on a particularly loud Hawaiian shirt with beach pants, came in the bedroom and announced, "Who's ready to go Arubaing?"

At the airport, Andrew made it a point to always have a carry-on bag in front of him and bought a newspaper to keep in his lap to hide his dimensions. They made it to the hotel and Allison rushed to get into her bikini. Then she threw Andrew a small gift-wrapped package. Andrew said, "What's this?"

"Open it and you'll see." To Andrew's horror it was a pair of Speedos matching her bikini. "I want everyone to know we're together."

Allison said, "It'll look so cute with your new pot belly." Andrew turned pale and sheepishly said, "You knew?"

Allison said of course she did. She was so flattered that he went to such great lengths to conceal it from her that she didn't feel any guilt about not mentioning her three-month affair with Wendell.

- I think of it as another of my erogenous zones.

- According to Freud, you're suffering from Pot Belly Envy.

> ### Toolbox Tips to Control Your Pot Belly
> Doctors have many ways for you to deal with your pot belly. Here's an easy one. You should begin a vigorous exercise program. You should also stop eating every food that you enjoy and become a meager-portion eating Vegan who nobody wants to eat with. You should definitely stop drinking any form of alcohol. At this point, the problem of not having sex will pale by comparison to the larger problem of dealing with your new found depression.

- I try to do everything that Buddha did.

- It's a guy thing. I wouldn't expect a *woman* to understand.

- I do tons of sit-ups. Underneath there's a six pack

- Most people would kill to have my low center of gravity.

- Are you anti-jolly?

The Pot Belly – Coat Camouflage

Figure 4: The Coat Camouflage

- If I exercised all the time, we'd never be together.

- Now that I've met you, I finally have a reason to lose it.

> **The Bad Sex Manual Hall of Fame**
> - It runs in my family.
> - My mother is Jewish/ Italian (Choose One).

Toolbox Tips to Control Your Pot Belly – Distraction

The art of distraction goes back thousands of hears. It is a little known fact that Cleopatra had a big belly, but few people ever noticed it because she always carried a beautiful, venomous snake with her. It was so deadly that people were afraid to take their eyes off it. Since she kept it next to her beautiful face, they just assumed she was gorgeous all over. This also accounted for the fact that she almost always reached an orgasm, while her partners rarely did.

Try this. When you are on a date, compliment her on the way she makes eye contact. Let her know that it makes her appear charming, intelligent and stunning. In the event that she loses focus and her eyes begin to drift south toward your midsection, quickly point away from yourself and say, "Look at that." It's way safer than holding a deadly snake.

Clinical Recommendations: Pot Belly
1. Camouflage your stomach with clothing
2. Darken the room
3. Divert her arms from the abdominal region
4. Assume the bottom sexual position

The Pot Belly – Sports Camouflage

Figure 4: The Sports Camouflage

Thing To Avoid for Men with Pot Bellies
1. Swimming Pools and Beaches
2. Hot tubs
3. Food
4. Any outfit with less than two layers
5. Women with keen eyesight
6. Thin women
7. Athletic women
8. Athletic Friends
9. Gyms
10. April to October

The Case of Frank K.

Frank loves food. He is a food connoisseur and dines at the finest restaurants. He is also a gourmet cook. He also appreciates junk food, greasy food and even the kind of food they get people to eat on Reality TV shows so they can remain on an island. He just loves food. Frank also has a vast collection of belts. These go along with his vast collection of pants. Both chronicle his love of food. It is an ever-growing collection. His friends tease him about his girth and he takes it good naturedly, but he does have a problem when he goes out on a date. Fear and embarrassment are not the cornerstones of a good potential relationship.

Treatment 1: The therapist suggested that Frank go on a diet.

Treatment 2: His new therapist suggested that Frank date only overweight women. This worked partially. He got along well with them, had plenty of dates, but there was one problem. They couldn't get their genitals and he never got to achieve penetration.

What he can say when...
she sees *his unample endowment.*
(*Little things don't always mean a lot.*)

Chapter 4B: Physical Attributes The Small Organ

Responses for Small Organ Size

- It's just the cold weather.

- It just looks small in this light.

- It's bigger than yours.

- Women aren't the only ones who have Penis Envy.

- I told you I wore a size 7 shoe.

- It looks small, but it weighs a lot.

- On a diet, everyone loses weight from someplace different.

- When you said you had three words for me I was expecting "I love you," not, "Is it in?"

Toolbox Tips to deal with an underdeveloped organ – Enlargement

Doctors now give you a choice. You can have pills, pumps, and surgeries and perform exercises. You can also learn to chant, meditate, take vitamins and hire people to tell you it looks bigger. If any of those methods worked, we would no longer be able to make fun of Japanese stereotypes and that would be a terrible loss for those of us who make ourselves feel better at others' expense. As our Asian friends sometimes say, "No workee."

- It only seems small compared to your beauty and charm.

- You've seen the bad news. The good news is I'll never hurt you.

- Please don't say, "OOooh, it's so cute!"

- You bet I'm insulted. I show you my baby picture and all you can say is, "You haven't changed a bit."

- I've been in the tub for almost an hour.

- Wait, did I just hear you say, "You're hurting me?"

- It's not really that small. Try looking at it from a different angle

- I donated most of it to charity.

- It *is* erect!

- Go on...laugh at it. Everyone else does.

- Maybe I need a woman with tiny breasts. She'll understand.

- I know it's a shock because I have big feet.

Little Known Bad Sex Facts: Sir Isaac Newton had one of the biggest breakthroughs in mathematics when he co-discovered calculus, and an even bigger breakthrough when he formulated the operational rules of gravity. He was very big above the shoulders, but not very big below the waist. Historian D. Winstead Parsons documented that Newton had one of the smallest penises in history of the Royal Academy of Science, but he was very good at measuring it.

Physical Predictors of Organ Size

1. Shoe Size
2. Hand Size
3. Nose Size
4. Lip Thickness
5. Height
6. Tongue Length
7. Weight

Table 1: Physical predictors of Men's Organ size (Ranked from High-to-low)

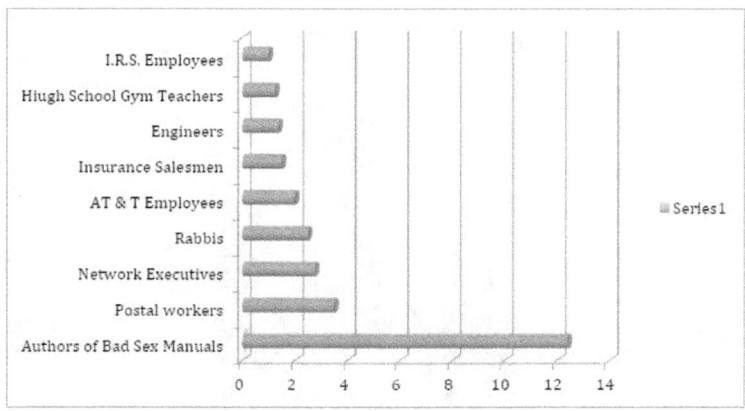

Table 2: Penis size (by occupation)

- You haven't seen what I can do with it yet.

- This is only the tip of the iceberg?

- How come you asked me why I drove a Porsche?

Pant and Sleeve Length are Good Predictors

Figure 1: Short Pant and Sleeve Length are Good Predictors of an Undersize Organ

- Not all of us have high voices.

- I'll be in and out before you even know it.

- If it's really your first time, how do you know that it's too small?

> **The Bad Sex Manual Hall of Fame**
> - It's not what you've got, but what you've got behind it.
> - Good things come in small packages.

Clinical Recommendations: Small Organ
1. Think Big
2. Always carry a briefcase, newspaper or other object in front of you.
3. Avoid public showers
4. Date very small women

Thing To Avoid for Men with Under-Endowment
1. Speedos
2. Tight pants
3. Locker rooms
4. Any woman who with a dress size larger than 2
5. Public bathrooms
6. Bright lights

> **The Case of Hideko W.**
> Hideko was small down there, even by Japanese standards. He refused to shower in public or change in locker rooms. He took to stuffing socks into his underwear. He also tried stuffing his underwear with various foods like zucchini and sausages, but several clashes with neighborhood dogs drove him back to his hamper. Hideko was smart, charming and witty, but as soon as he seemed to be hitting it off with a woman, he was certain that she was casting furtive glances southward.

Treatment 1: Against therapeutic advice, Hideko, who loved late night television, tried a plethora of enlargement pills, supplements and mechanical devices. In a sad word, he found *little* results.

Treatment 2: His therapist had Hideko study the Kama Sutra and experiment with positions where he could optimize his size. After a few tries, he met with no success and refused to continue treatment. His chiropractor, who he now visits three times a week because of position #12 (Monkey Woman Under Tree Bark), agrees with Hideko's decision to stop Kama Sutraing.

Treatment 3: His therapist suggested that he pursue women who are radically different from the ones he'd been seeing. He suggested three specific types of women. Ones that were tiny in stature, had serious eyesight deficiencies, particularly myopia and ones who were enormously gullible. We will report on the results as they come in.

Teaching Stories
Eleanor Learns How Size Matters

Eleanor had recurring sexual nightmares. And they were all theme and variations on the same subject. She would awaken in a cold sweat every night after a dismal dream about having sex with a man who had a small penis.

Each night when she went on a date, she was careful to sensually brush up against the man three or four times until she could see the size of his erection. If she wasn't sure, she would trip and as she fell, brush it slowly to get a more accurate digital measurement.

Unable to stand it anymore, Eleanor made an appointment with her therapist. He had already diagnosed her with Petitofalusophobia. This is an irrational fear of small phalluses. He suggested that she should think about escaping from her dreams by taking an extravagant trip. "Go someplace exotic where you've never been before." She immediately went on the Internet and started to do careful research on exotic locations and their corresponding member size. After extensive research, she settled in the Island of Fiji. It was a popular tourist site, but not overly built-up like Hawaii or Tahiti. And, oh... the size of the men. And we're not talking about height or weight.

She was shown to her first class seat next to Sam. He was in his mid 30s. Sam was average looking. After a few hours, Sam fell asleep and must have been having one of those dreams because he had an erection. Eleanor laughed and thought it was barely enough to be called an erectionette. But her spirits were in no way dampened because once she set foot on Fiji, Sam would be a small, very small memory.

As Eleanor was dozing off, there was a bit of turbulence on the jet, and it began to shake just a little. Then it subsided for a few minutes, and then it shook thunderously. Oxygen masks fell, life vests were inflated, and Eleanor wished she had paid better attention to the safety movie. The last thing she remembered before waking up on a small raft alone with Sam was nothing.

After a day and a half of drifting, they saw land. Having no oars, they had to use their hands to paddle, but they made it to shore exhausted, but they made it. As Eleanor lay there clutching her chest and trying to catch her breath, Sam was already exploring the tiny island. It took him less than 12 minutes because it was just a tiny atoll, But it had a coconut tree with coconuts on it and an ocean full of seafood waiting to be caught.

Sam was quite handy and figured out how to catch fish and being a former boy scout, he even knew how to start a fire. On their first night, they dined under the stars on fish, coconut meat and coconut milk. After a week of exchanging biographies and eating their monotonous diets they finally got around to a kiss. Eleanor immediately remembered Sam's sleeping state. She freaked out and said she needed to take a walk by herself. Her nightmares had come true in the worst way possible. If she had a one-night stand with a small man, she could just never see him again. If she dated a small man, she could break up with him. Even if she had married a small man, she could divorce him. But being stuck on a deserted desert island, and a beautifully romantic one at that dammit, and he was literally the last man on that earth... what was she going to do? What could she do?

Part of her wanted to give it a try. It was almost two weeks since her last fling, but he was so tiny. It would be the death of hope and the beginning of her lifelong nightmare. One she had already begun living through every night. At the same time, she began wondering why after two weeks, why hasn't he made a move? Did he not find her attractive? No, that's impossible. Was he gay? No, she had good Gaydar. And he would have already talked about how most of the big actors in Hollywood were gay. So many of them like to do that. Was he asexual? Wait, was he embarrassed about his size? What to do?

She decided to go back, try a little more kissing and say that they should go real slow. The French said the best part of love was the chase. And, they certainly weren't going anywhere. She went back. They kissed. And it was not bad. Hell, it was pretty good. Was it really good, or was she just horny? More questions to be answered.

By the sixth night, they were dry humping, even though it was a very humid night and it was hard to keep anything dry. Then to keep the romantic mood alive, they began questioning each other's sexual history. "When did you have your last AIDS test? How many sexual partners have you had in your life? How well did you know each of them?"

These questions may have broken the magic moment that only dry humping can create, but they did finally decide that they were both appropriate candidates for coitus. For the first time in three weeks, Eleanor tried to use her cell phone to call her therapist. Not surprisingly, because she had a four-year contract with AT & T, she found no reception. Damn. It sure would have been nice to talk to Dr. Williams. She never referred to him as her "shrink" for obvious reasons.

Well, she decided that tonight would be the night. They slowly undressed each other, which didn't take long since they wore only a few rags anyway. Eleanor couldn't bear to look down. She got up for a second and put out the fire. That night there was only a sliver of moon. She could barely see it, and she knew why that was. As she was about to reach for it, Sam said, Eleanor, there's something I have to tell you. Having read *The Bad Sex Manual*, Eleanor clenched her jaws and waited for the line. Boy was she surprised.

"I was born very well-endowed. Other men envied me, but they had no idea of the trouble it caused me. I had women stalking me all the time. Every night I would come home and my voice-mailbox was full. I got texts, emails even faxes. It just got to be too much. I was the target of women at work. I could barely walk down the street without women undressing me with their eyes. So I went to see Dr. Dworkin."

"Dr. Dworkin is a world-class plastic surgeon with a specialization in urologic reconstruction. His specialization was penis reduction surgery. I had the surgery done almost a year ago. He told me that the procedure was reversible within a one-year span. That means I have one week to go and the window closes. That's why I planned this trip to Fiji now so that I couldn't possibly be tempted. Once in a while it was nice, but most of the time it was a horror show. Yes, two thirds of me is cryogenically frozen at Johns Hopkins University and will be disposed of by next week at this time."

Eleanor jumped up and started running. After she got a few hundred feet away from Sam, she screamed out at the heavens. "God, really? This is how you're going to play it? Was I really that bad a person? OK, I fudged a few 1090 IRS forms, and I overestimated a few Goodwill contributions, but c'mon. I give money to homeless people, I give up my seat on the subway to old people. I'm a good person. Why?"

When she got back, she saw that Sam restarted the fire and was asleep next to it. She laid down next to him and softly cried herself to sleep. Then she started to think and a word popped into her head. A magic word that could be the key that unlocked her golden door...LESBIANS. They seem happy and they don't even have little ones. She slowly reached around, found what was left of Sam's pants. Rubbed what was left inside them. They had disappointingly mediocre sex. Two days later they were rescued and she flew back to the city, never having sampled the size of Fijian men. Sam stayed on Fiji until his week was up then happily went home.

Did Eleanor learn anything from this experience and her subsequent visit to Dr. Williams? Yes, and it can be summed up in a single word...Ambien.

Part Two: For Women

Introduction

None of the aspects of Bad Sex mentioned in this text have occurred to the women known by the authors (at least during the time they were with the authors). As with the Men's Volume, the information presented here is based on the data gathered by the authors.

We would like to thank the many women who helped the authors (Including the ones who had no idea they were helping them during that help). As with the Men's Volume, this part of the text should help restore the nation back to a proper level of mental health. In addition, the data presented here should shed light on the foremost questions facing sex researchers today.

There are two major schools of thought regarding women's sexuality:

1. One school believes that women *never* enjoy sex.
2. The other school believes that women *always* enjoy it.

Our research bears directly on this issue. We discovered that if women experience Bad Sex, and realize that it is bad, then they must occasionally experience Non-Bad Sex. How else would they know the difference? Therefore, Good and Bad Sex must *both* exist. Even though this flies in the face of what many girls told us in high school, we believe that we have proven our point unequivocally.

What she can say when...
she didn't, but should have.
(The cold hard facts.)

Chapter 5: Frigidity

Responses for Explaining Frigidity

- I think I may have. I'm not sure.

- I told you to blow in my ear cause it turns me on … not blow out my eardrum.

- If you had been a real man, you would have made me have it.

- What do you care? You got yours.

- You were so good it scared me.

- I just got distracted watching you enjoying yourself.

- I was sooooo close a few times.

- I can't let go with a man I've only known for three months.

- Can you prove that I didn't?

- It doesn't help asking "Didja, huh, Didja?"

Tension is an indicator of Frigidity

Figure 1: Tension is a warning sign of **Bad Sex** – Frigidity

- I told you I had a headache.

- When you said, "What does this part do?" I got a bit distracted.

- I have just as much right *not to* as any man does.

- First of all, you shouldn't have brought your copy of *Sex for Dummy's*. Worse, your bookmark is on page 9.

- The good news is I feel less guilty about cheating on my husband.

- You're supposed to say, "I love you" during, not after.

- Maybe the twelve seconds of foreplay wasn't enough.

- How come I didn't and you're the one who says he's frustrated?

> ### Toolbox Tips to Control Frigidity – Blaming
>
> Psychologists suggest that the first step in overcoming frigidity is to identify its cause. This can take a long time and still not lead to a satisfactory solution. The key to dealing with frigidity is to simply blame your partner and say you can't change until they do. Blaming, or to use its technical name, Causal Transference, is virtually foolproof and it works almost instantly. If your partner shows any signs of resistance, simply point your finger directly at your partner and say, "See, you've just made my point."

- **CHOOSE ONE OF THE FOLLOWING:**

It's the same cologne my _____ wore.
   ___ a. father
   ___ b. old boyfriend
   ___ c. old girlfriend

- You're the first one.

- I was saving it for your birthday. It was going to be a surprise.

- Some of those things you made me do were disgusting.

Inducing Sympathy to Mask Frigidity

Figure 2: Masking Frigidity by Inducing Sympathy from the partner

- I was afraid if you saw me let go, you'd think I was an animal.

- It's not because you're too small... really.

- I think your drooling caught me by surprise.

- Maybe if you take off your pants and shirt?

- Oh, my last boyfriend assured me that most women never do.

> ### Toolbox Tips to Control Frigidity – Testosterone and Estrogen Manipulation
>
> Endocrinologists believe that they can treat frigidity by tampering with the delicate balance of these two mysterious hormones. If you are gullible enough to think this may work, just ask around to see how sexually satisfied the wives of most endocrinologists are.

- Would you mind saying, "Now it's time for Daddy's little girl to sit down on Daddy's lap and wiggle?"

- I'm used to men who are, how can I put this…masculine.

- The nuns told us if we enjoyed it too much, we'd burn in Hell for eternity.

- Did it occur to you that there's more than one way to take "Who's your daddy?"

- You know, it makes me feel worse when you look so sad.

- If I wasn't so liberated, I'd cry.

- Don't feel bad…even though I do blame you.

- If you want, I can fake it…just like the last few times.

Key Words and Phrases that Indicate Bad Sex

Young Republicans	My Doctor Says	I'm Not Supposed To	Quick
Fast	I can't	Small	Oops
Headache	Oh No!	Headache	Oh No!
Tired	Sorry	Limp	Sluggish

Table 1: Indicators of Bad Sex

Handshakes as Indicators

Men	Women
The handshake is over too quickly	Her hand is cold
His handshake is too limp	She doesn't arch her wrist
His hand is damp and clammy	She is reluctant to shake hands
His hand is too small	She digs her nails into your hand
He says, "Ow, that hurts."	She says, "Not now, I've got a headache"

Table 2: Handshakes as Indicators of Bad Sex

Blaming the Partner

Figure 3: Blaming the Partner to divert attention away from frigidity

- You know "inexperienced" doesn't mean "clueless."

- The second hour of dry humping chaffed me.

> ### Toolbox Tips to Control Frigidity – Affection
> Another suggestion for dealing with frigidity is that partners employ some of the following strategies: increase hugging, caressing, complimenting, passionate kissing, using affectionate terms, expressing their love and making you feel wanted and special. Frankly, it's easy to see the gender of the person who came up with these solutions. Furthermore, it sounds like someone who just didn't know how to spell the word "alcohol."

Occupational Groups with the Highest Rate of Frigidity

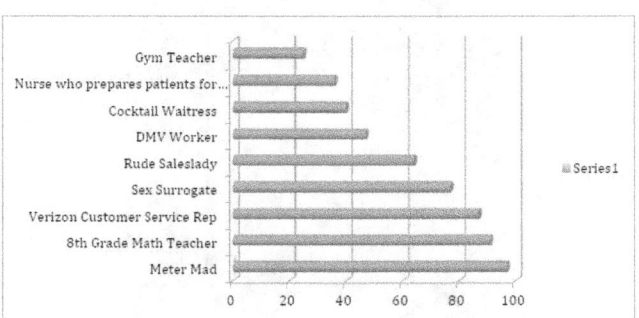

Table 3: Occupational Groups with the Highest Percentage of Frigidity

- You should have let me take that Xanax.

- I get self-conscious with the lights on.

- Can you reach my phone, I want to call my therapist?

- I'm not frigid. I'm reserved.

Frigid Woman during sex

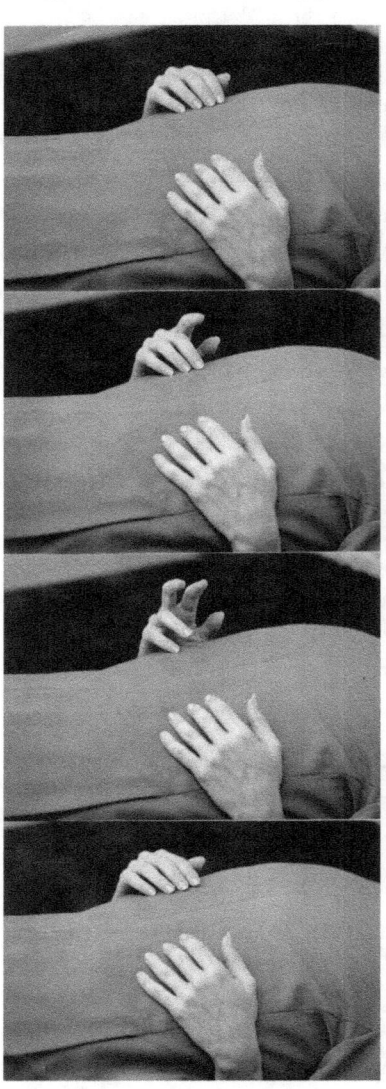

Figure 4: Time lapse Photo of a Frigid Woman during sex

Peter Desberg, Ph.D. and Tom McLoughlin Ph.D.less

Teaching Stories
Wendy Comes to Terms with her Frigidity

Albert lives in Jacksonville Florida and it's hot. Not New York in the summer hot, but really hot. It's hot in Albert's car, it's hot in his apartment, but not in his bed. Albert's wife is frigid.

When they went out in high school, he got to second base and she was breathing heavy so he was sure she was turned on. Truth be told, her breathing was the result of pushing Albert away so they wouldn't get to third base, plus guilt, plus Jacksonville. It's hot there.

They got married right out of high school and on their wedding night, Albert was ready. His first cue should have been that it took Wendy half an hour to come out of the bathroom and then it took ten minutes to take off all the layers of bathrobes, nighties and lingerie she was swathed in. But he didn't notice a thing. Five years of sexual longing and frustration can do that to a young, hormonal boy.

They kissed and as she touched his thigh, he exploded into his first sexual experience ... a pre-premature ejaculation. Wendy kissed him on the cheek, told him they had consummated their marriage and immediately rolled over and feigned sleep. By the time he changed into fresh pajamas, there was nothing for him to do but wait for the next night.

On the second night of their honeymoon, he managed to achieve penetration for 8 seconds before erupting again. By the end of the honeymoon, Albert sensed that there may be a problem here.

One night, Albert climbed into bed with Wendy, made his typical opening move and was rejected again. Third night in a row. He decided it was time to talk. Wendy was reluctant, but finally explained that she was raised with the idea that sex was dirty and only to be endured with a husband for the purpose of having children. Albert climbed out of bed, went into the other room and used the Internet for a bit of satisfaction. And so it went for the next three months, until Albert arrived home from work early.

He heard a strange noise coming from their bedroom. It sounded like moaning, but it was Wendy's voice. It was hard to put those two things together. He tiptoed up to the door, which was open a crack and peeked in. There was Wendy in bed with a 12 inch black rubber vibrating dildo. She was gyrating and moaning and after watching this scene for five minutes, he got so turned on that he burst into the room, but the only sound that he could manage was, "Aha."

Wendy screamed, threw down the dildo and quickly put on her bathrobe. It was still on the floor vibrating as Wendy was crying hysterically. She threw some clothes in the car and left for three days. No calls, no texts...nothing.

When she finally returned home she said, "If you say a word about it, I'm leaving for good." The next two weeks were the most awkward of Albert's life. He felt angry, he felt betrayed, he felt frustrated and he was so turned on.

Finally, he went up to Wendy and said it wasn't fair. He demanded to have her listen to one word. She figured that would be safe. Albert's word was, "counseling." Wendy reluctantly agreed. The first twenty minutes was a torrent of words that Albert had been storing up for quite a while, but the counselor was able to piece together what happened. She turned to Wendy and said, "What's your side of the story?"

Wendy began, "Everything that Albert said is true. And Albert is so nice. I cry myself to sleep each night knowing that I'm not satisfying him, but I just don't feel anything down there when we try to get romantic. I love him so much and he's so nice and that just makes me feel really bad." Then she finished talking abruptly with the word "bad" just hanging around for everyone in the room to take in.

Then the counselor asked about the elephant in the room, or in this case, the elephant dildo in the room. Wendy turned red, her breathing quickened she looked around, was about to talk, then abruptly stopped. The counselor put her hand on Wendy's shoulder. Wendy jerked herself away and screamed, "And I'm not gay, if you think that's my problem." She ran out of the room and waited for Albert in the car.

After quite a lot of persuasion, she agreed to try counseling again, but with a different counselor. They went through the same story and once again stopped when she said she felt bad, but this time, when she got to the word "bad" she smiled just a little. Both Albert and the counselor noticed and asked her about it. Wendy got mad. She got up to go, but this time Albert grabbed her by the arm and pushed her back down on the couch.

Wendy grabbed Albert and kissed him passionately and talking a mile-a-minute. She said, "Albert has always been so nice that the idea of sex made me feel unclean. I never got turned on. But when I used to think about how bad I was to him, I got turned on. I would rub myself on the corners of the table until I discovered vibrators. Of course I couldn't tell Albert because... he was just so nice." Just now, when he grabbed me, I felt aroused by him for the first time. If you don't mind, we're going home to take care of some unfinished business."

Albert and Wendy had sex every night for seven months before their divorce. Once he realized that Wendy liked bad boys, he became one. A far worse one than Wendy had ever dreamed of. He now hangs out with his new motorcycle club and she is on match.com looking for a moderately bad boy.

- I might have underestimated the effect of you being my Gynecologist.

- We can still salvage it ... three minutes with my vibrator.

Body Temperatures during Sex Cycle

	Excitement	Plateau	Orgasm	Resolution
Normal	98.6	99	99.2	98.7
Frigid	98.6	97.4	No Data available	97.8

Table 4: Body Temperature of Normal and Frigid women during the 4 stages of Sex Cycle

Little Known Bad Sex Facts: Have you ever noticed that the Mona Lisa smile is a bit cold? That's because she was frigid. Da Vinci had been dating her for some time and thought that a flattering portrait might warm her up a bit. It did nothing. (*Excuse the marks on the photo, but since we are revealing some sensitive material, the Vinci family would only release the rights if we let them use their watermark on the photo they sent us*).

Confusing the Partner by Acting Smug

Figure 5: Acting smug to confuse partner

- I didn't *not have* one on purpose.

- I think it has something to do with the fact that you kept calling me Susie. My name is Carol.

- I held back because I just changed the sheets.

> **The Bad Sex Manual Hall of Fame**
> - I was so close.
> - I'm afraid I'll get pregnant.
> - Your hands were too cold.
> - You intimidate me.

Clinical Recommendations: Frigidity
1. Begin moaning slowly.
2. Increase your moaning speed.
3. Slowly begin to raise the speed of your moaning.
4. Arch your back.
5. Scream the name of any deity you believe in (If you don't believe in one, scream out your partner's name, but don't expect the same level of acceptance).
6. Pant for 12.8 seconds.
7. Stop moving and close your eyes and say, "Incredible" in the lowest pitched voice you can manage.
8. Do nothing else, but lay there for at least 9 minutes. (If he attempts to talk, or question you, place your index finger over his mouth and say, "Shhhhh.")
9. Whenever you have a spare moment, use your peripheral vision to look at calendars of shirtless fireman.

Thing To Avoid for Women who are Frigid
1. Avoid weak men
2. Avoid strong men
3. Don't make eye contact
4. Stay out of air conditioned buildings

The Case of Betty K.

As a child, Betty K. always called her mom to bring in an extra blanket before she could fall asleep. Her friends at school called her "Betty Muffler" because she wore them nine months out of each year. But Betty was considered a friendly girl, just not too friendly.

Betty was always a good girl. And she was such a high achiever. She won more badges in Girls Scouts, sold more magazines to help feed the poor and was easily the smartest girl in Bible study. She lived a quiet, stress-free life until that Thursday night phone call.

A boy in her class named Billy asked her to be his date for the 8th grade dance. They went, they danced and went to the party after at Jane's house. Betty knew that Billy and Jane ran with the fast-lane popular kids. It was something she always hoped to try, but didn't think it was in the cards for her. What a night, until he drove her home. She was hoping he

would give her a good night kiss... her first. She laid her head back on the car seat, closed her eyes and waited. But she was not prepared for what happened next.

He didn't start with his lips. Before she realized what was happening, his hands were in a place where they definitely shouldn't have been. She jumped straight up, slammed her head on the roof of his car and ran into her house trying to catch her breath, hide her tears and think about what she would offer at Confession the next day.

Fast forward six years and nothing fast, or slow happened again.

Treatment 1: The therapist suggested that she accept a date with a boy whom she could talk to openly. She would explain everything and finally get her kiss. And from there, move slowly, very slowly to see where things would eventually go. The only boy she could find that was willing was a nerdy boy name William. The minute they had their first kiss in the car, William ran out and looked for a therapist to help with his new found Premature Ejaculation problem.

Treatment 2: The therapist suggested that Betty begin a desensitization experiment using a small vibrator. This way she could go at her own pace and keep her anxiety level low. Three years later, Betty owns seven vibrators of increasing sizes and strengths. She gave each one a name and plans to call William again soon.

What she can say when...
she does, and he doesn't.
(This actually Happens)

Chapter 6: Unstimulating

Responses for when this actually does happen...

- If you really wanted to, you would have.

- Are you sure that men only have one type of orgasm?

- You looked so tired, I figured we'd better stop and get some rest.

- Maybe next time it'll be your turn.

- ...and you were in such a hurry to get started.

- Did I dig my nails into your back too hard?

- Are you sure you didn't? Check that condom again.

- You showed incredible restraint.

- I didn't either, I just faked it.

- Do you want to see if you can do any better with my sister?

- Don't you ever pray that you'll have an orgasm.

Diverting Attention Through Cuteness

Figure 1: Diversion Through Cuteness

- Are you threatened by strong women?

- If you wanna' to go into the bathroom with my laptop... I'll understand.

- Does that cigarette mean you're given up?

- Are you afraid that if you did, I'd take it as a sign of commitment?

- Did it bother you when I couldn't stop laughing?

- If you refuse to concentrate, there's not much I can do.

- Are you holding back to tease me?

- I don't think any less of you because you didn't.

- Let's go to sleep. Maybe you'll have a nocturnal emission.

> ### Toolbox Tips to Control His Satisfaction
> Begin by accepting full responsibility. This will make it easier for you to change. First find out what his fantasies and fetishes are. A good way to do this is to look for his bookmarks on pornography websites. If all else fails, ask him. If that fails, get him high and ask him. Once you find out... do it... do it all. Don't ask questions, just do it.

- Want to take a peek at my new Victoria's Secret catalogue?

- Do you have this trouble often?

- Someday you'll want me to, then see if I do!!!

- A real man would have already.

- Is it because I'm too wholesome and you're used to sleazier women?

Word Associations of individuals who regularly experience Bad Sex

Men		Women	
Stimulus	Response	Stimulus	Response
Slow	Fast	Touch	Don't
Hard	Soft	Hot	Cold
Thin	Fat	Climax	Can't
Yes	No	Sex	Burden
Over	Quickly	69	70
Climax	Dammit	Multiple Orgasm*	(No Response)
Firm	Rarely	Penetrate	Ouch
Woman	Castrate	Penis	Ouch
Ball	Break	Man	Friction

Table 1: Word Associations of individuals who experience Bad Sex

- Please Try!

- Are you mad at me?

- Are you still afraid of your mother?

- Well, at least one of us had fun.

- Do you have ADD?

- It'll be so intense when you finally do.

- Do you realize how hostile you're being?

---

* Several women asked us to repeat this phrase then define it.

- Could be worse. You could have been premature. *(Author's Note: Then we'd have to go back to Chapter 1.)*

- Maybe you're feeling guilty because you took me to a cheap restaurant.

Diverting Attention by Acting Like a Mysterious Stranger

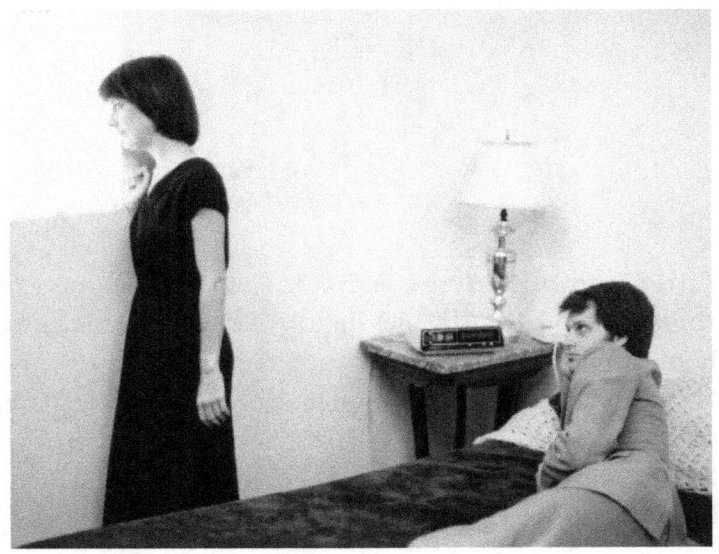

Figure 2: Distraction by acting like a mysterious stranger

- Maybe you're frigid?

- You really hate women, don't you?

- Maybe you have to pee...and you don't know it

Little Known Bad Sex Facts: Cleopatra, daughter of the Sun God Ra, did, while all of the men pictured behind her didn't. And this was a common occurrence. It could have been her famed lack of personal hygiene, or the threat that if she didn't, they would be thrown into a snake pit. Nevertheless, she was renowned for finishing well while her partners didn't.

Teaching Story
Vera Did

Vera believed the song "All The Girls Get Prettier At Closing Time" was written about her. She wasn't ugly, but you wouldn't call her pretty. Neither did most men. She wasn't fat, but she could stand to lose a few pounds. If ten women were standing around, she'd be the seventh one you'd notice. To make up for her physical shortcomings, she wasn't a sparkling conversationalist either. But Vera was resilient. No matter how many failed attempts she had, she was always on the lookout for the next "Mr. Right," even though it seemed that both he and luck seemed to avoid her.

She tried lots of strategies until she found the one that worked for her. Hit the bars 45 minutes before Last Call. At this point, the great looking ones have already been whisked out and the grungy ones had been picked over and rejected. Compared to them, she looked pretty good, and she was "fresh meat."

She compiled a list of 42 bars that catered to the type of guys she liked and they were geographically desirable. Since she didn't go prowling every night, it took her around three months to go through the list and start again. That helped her to maintain her anonymity and kept every visit a bit tingly.

After completing a series of online self-improvement classes, Vera learned the secret to slightly increasing the probability of a bit of happiness. Lower Your Expectations. So each night that she managed to bring someone home, the goal was not to have discovered Mr. Right, but to get a call back asking for a date. One day, as she was calculating her average callbacks, which was at around 29%, she began reflecting on her recent copular history.

Having very few sexual inhibitions, Vera always climaxed... always. But, she noticed that quite a few of the men she had been with hadn't. Looking in the mirror, she immediately accepted all the blame and attributed it to her looks. After a few short weeks of debilitating depression, she thought she should look into it. She hit on the idea of calling her previous partners and interviewing them to see if she could figure out what was going on.

James
When James looked at his phone and saw Vera's name he panicked. He had seen her twice, realized that it wasn't happening

and moved on. He reasoned that this call could only contain bad news. Being the type of guy that rips the Band-Aid off rapidly, he took her call. Jumbled thoughts of pregnancy, STDs and crabs flew through his mind as Vera offered him a very strange proposal. She asked if she could take him out to lunch and talk about the sex they had, with the understanding that they would never do it again.

All of a sudden, James had a few hot thoughts about Vera, but agreed to lunch anyway. Maybe he could order the forbidden fruits on the menu. Vera went right to the heart of the matter and opened with, "Why didn't you come when we had sex?"

James scratched his head and said, "Are you sure? I usually do." Vera assured him that he didn't and she wanted to know why. As he thought back to the bar where he met her, he smiled and said, "Yeh, now I remember. It was really late at night and I was really wasted." He was no help.

Brian
Just like every guy who received a Vera lunch request, Brian went through the same list of fears at seeing her name pop up on her phone. Like James, all Brian could come up with were the twin excuses of late and drunk.

Michael
Just as Vera was thinking this wasn't such a good idea, Michael picked up the phone. He jumped at the chance to have lunch and took it one step farther. He asked to make it dinner at his place and he would cook. Vera had made it abundantly clear that sex was off the table. Even if she wasn't engaged, her curiosity was. She didn't dress up for the occasion. After all, it was five hours before closing time and this wasn't a bar.

As they sat down to dinner, before she could get a word out, Michael insisted that she try some of the exquisite vodka he had in his freezer. Being polite she accepted the drink. The next five shots came from a different place than politeness, but who's counting when it goes down so smooth.

Before she could ask her question, they were already under the sheets. After her third orgasm, her breathing became steady enough to notice that she was once again the only one on the climax train. She ran into the bedroom and came out wearing his bathrobe and began crying. It wasn't that late and they weren't that drunk. She cautiously asked what happened, and why he didn't.

Michael hedged, making it clear that he really didn't want to talk about it. But Vera was relentless. And the tears didn't hurt her cause either. So Michael began to explain that he was addicted to Internet Porn and it made regular sex kind of boring. He suggested that perhaps if she played the role of a young girl from Shanghai who was sent to clean his house and then ended up tying him up and having sex, maybe that would be enough to…

Vera threw her clothes on as quickly as she could to get away from this freak. Running through streets with cold damp hair felt exhilarating. She was visited by a clarity she had never experienced before. What she had to do was find bars with poorer lighting and begin earlier in the evening.

- I thought you were more competitive. Doesn't it bother you to finish last, or not at all?

- Look on the bright side, we've both burned a lot of calories.

Breakdown of People With Whom Women Talk About Bad Sex

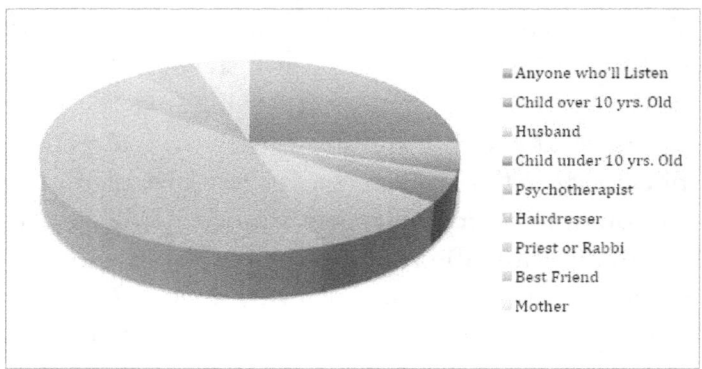

Table 2: A percentage breakdown of the People Whom Women Talk About Bad Sex

- We're not quitting until you do.

- If you're holding back for my sake, you don't have to any more.

- Just remember, you owe me one.

- Why does it have to be anyone's fault?

- Sometimes you act as if you'd never been an adolescent.

Diverting Attention by Pretending to be Asleep

Figure 3: Diversion by pretending to be asleep

- I'm impressed by your restraint. Now prove it was by choice.

- Was it the garlic?

- I always heard that this could happen, but I never expected it to happen to me.

- You're too paranoid about getting me pregnant. Take off one of those condoms.

- Most men would dream of being able to go this long.

- Maybe you should eat more red met.

> **The Bad Sex Manual Hall of Fame**
> - I hope my screaming didn't bother you.
> - I didn't know you were so ticklish.
> - You don't think I'm pretty enough.

Clinical Recommendations: She Does He Doesn't
1. Explain that "Real Men" always do.
2. Talk to him about the concept of Alternative Gender Preference and let him know that you support it and voted for Same Sex Marriage.

Thing To Avoid for Women who did when their partners didn't
1. Avoid gloating
2. Avoid taking a victory lap
3. Avoid eye contact
4. Avoid Guilt

The Case of Bianca M.

Bianca was never considered shy by anyone. She was friendly, smart and always a go-getter. She got good grades. She was popular in school. After college she got a good job. All because she knew what she wanted and went after it. This trait also extended to men ... sort of.

No one ever accused Bianca of being coy. If she liked a guy, she let him know it. If she wanted to kiss him, or pet with him, she did. You can see where this is going. And Bianca was a finisher. After a while, Bianca noticed a terrible trend. When she went to bed with a man, more often than not, she would finish, of course, but he wouldn't.

Treatment 1: The therapist suggested that perhaps Bianca pay a little more attention to her partner in bed. She took this in and put it into action immediately. Every two or three minutes, she would ask, "Did you?" This strategy would work well in court for an interrogator, but it didn't produce the erotic outcome she was hoping for.

Treatment 2: Her therapist suggested that she ask her partners to abstain from sexual relations for a period of two months before they tried. After a six-month period, two of her partners had premature ejaculations and two of them were so nervous, they were unable to get aroused because of the tension.

What she can say when...
he wants to... and she doesn't.
(Say it isn't "no.")

Chapter 7: Just Say "NO"

Responses for Polite Refusals

- I can't sleep with every guy I meet. It looks like you're the one I don't sleep with.

- I know that it would be incredible, and I'd glow afterwards. My father would see my glow and shoot you.

- We're incompatible. You're Baptist and I like good-looking guys.

- I just don't think I could stand seeing you have such a good time.

- You're lucky to get a handshake after taking me out for a hotdog and a coke.

- Does this look like my YES face?

- I don't want to end up as just another of your tattoos.

- You didn't ask me nicely.

- I don't get the results back on my Herpes Test till tomorrow, but if you really want to…

- "I'm so horny" isn't really a turn on for me.

- Are you kidding? I'm a Libra and you're an Aries.

- It's not because I'm Black and you're White… I just don't like you.

- You didn't know that some women's periods can last 24 days a month?

- Do you really think whining makes you more attractive?

- We're friends without benefits.

- Do you really think whining makes you more attractive?

You Can Tell That She's Lying Cause She's Smiling

Figure 1: You can tell that she's lying because she is smiling

- The hair on your chest reminds me of my father.

- Too tired now...let's talk about it in the morning?

- You're friends with Frank, Frank will tell Pam, Pam will tell Jane and Jane will post it on her wall.

- The pit bulls might think you're attacking me.

- Here's the problem... you're not emotionally available and I'm not physically available.

- Sorry, but I forgot my diaphragm.

> ### Toolbox Tips to Control Rejection
> ### Making Them Think It's Their Fault
> Since men are only going out with you for one reason, and you both know it, let them know that you know it. Point out that you know why they listened to all your stories, agreed to eat sushi, complimented you on your new dress and told you that you are witty and intelligent. Let them know that you know it was just an act and that it won't work. Then just explain that you'll know when the time is right and you'll let them know.

- I'm riding the cotton pony.

- You *say* you love me, but how do I know you *really* love me?

- I'd have to shower first, it'll take two hours to blow dry my hair and put on my make up. By that time you may not be in the mood and I can't take the chance of being rejected.

You Can Tell That She's Lying Cause She Looks Sad

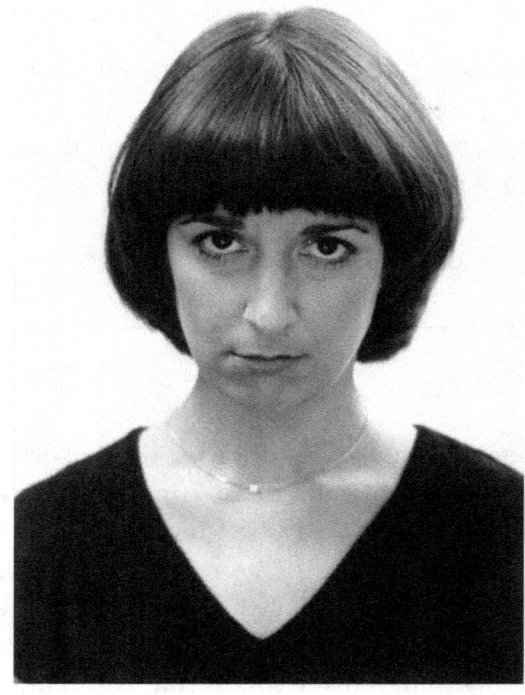

Figure 2: You can tell that she's lying because she looks sad

- I may be easy, but I'm not that easy.

- Hold on, whatever happened to kissing, foreplay... romance?

- Seriously? In the back seat of your Volvo?

- If you were the last man on earth we'd still have to negotiate.

Sexual Rejection by Occupation

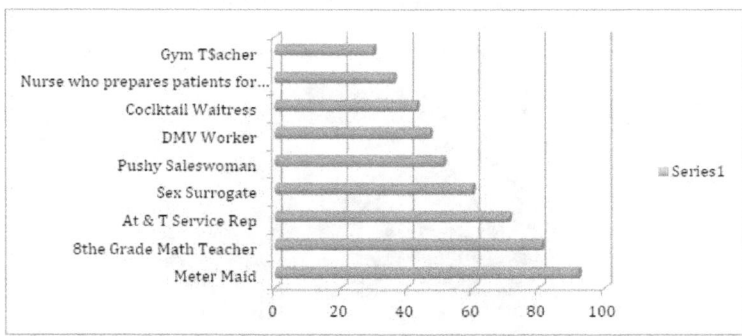

Table 1: Probability of being rejected by a potential sex partner by occupation

- Just because you're naked doesn't mean we're going to.

- "Shut up and spread 'em" isn't a romantic seduction ... even if it was imported beer.

- On one condition ... no touching.

- I promised my dying grandmother I would wait.

- It's got nothing to do with you. Well maybe it does.

You Can Tell That She's Lying Cause She Looks Seductive

Figure 3: You can tell that she's lying because she looks seductive

Teaching Stories
No Means No

Wilson was positive that he didn't like anything negative. And that went double for any person crossing his path. The only image he remembers from his childhood is hearing his parents yelling the word, "No." The context for the reprimand was almost irrelevant. Whatever he picked up, whatever he tried to do, someone was yelling, "Don't," or, "Stop!" Now, as a 29-year-old man, he still dreaded hearing his phone ring just on the off chance that it was one of his parents who were always ready to tell him where and how his life was going wrong. It didn't matter which parent, they were interchangeable when it came to being disapproving.

He tried to live his life with this over-arching philosophy, "Say 'Yes' whenever you can." He was kind, good natured, and well liked by all his friends...unless they said, "No," or were negative in any way. Then a voice seemed to pop into his head that says, "It's time to make a new friend."

As you might guess, this caused Wilson a problem or two when it came to dating. The natural give-and-take of picking a restaurant or a movie is commonplace for most people, but they are land mines to Wilson. So that's why he developed a very adaptive strategy for dealing with what we might refer to as his "eccentricity."

To avoid arguments and any negativity, he would simply ask the question first. She never knew she was in a race and he had the edge. If she returned a polite, "No, where would you like to go?" Or, "What would you like to do?" He would insist that she decide. So, on each date he asked what his date would like to do, where she'd like to eat, what movie to go to or even where to take a vacation if things got that far. Since he would agree to anything she said, no problems.

Well almost no problems. There is that crucial moment when a couple is in the beginning stages of dating, sexual excitement begins to peak, and, on occasion, the woman might still say "No." Wilson handled this with an adaptation of The Plan. Always lets the woman lead. Don't be in a hurry. You'll get there when the time is right. And this had worked work fairly well for the past three or four years, at least until he met Agnes.

Agnes
She was a graduate of both Our Leady of the Blessed Sacrament Catholic School and Notre Dame. Sixteen years of Catholic education, unless you counted Sunday Bible study. If you do, add two more years. She attended church fairly regularly and tried to lead a virtuous life. Agnes thought of herself as a "good" girl, using the standard most nuns used. Of course there had been a few bumps in the road along the way.

A few times she woke up on a Sunday morning at a frat house she didn't remember going to. Nor did she recognize the naked boy sleeping next to her. And over the years she had a few long-term relationships where bonds were consummated, but you'd never describe Agnes as promiscuous. Never. And every transgression, no matter whether it was enormous or slight was dutifully divulged at the first available confessional.

Wilson enjoyed his dates with Agnes, but he began to notice something that didn't feel quite right. Her path toward intimacy was quite a bit slower than his experience would have predicted. But he didn't want things to turn south so he waited patiently. Up to this point, they already kissed good night regularly, made out on the couch and they had even fallen asleep watching TV, but fully clothed. Wilson found himself getting a bit frustrated with this roadblock. He decided to turn up the heat a bit, and he couldn't have picked a worse time or woman to do it with.

Although Agnes never told Wilson anything about her ex-boyfriend Nick, she thought about him constantly, but not in a good way. Nick introduced her to some aspects of his culturally diverse background. Nick was Greek, and when they got physical, he had a gift for making Agnes feel dirty…very dirty.

She also didn't tell Wilson that they had broken up only days before she met him and this was a particularly confusing rebound relationship. She liked Wilson. That wasn't the problem. But she couldn't even get the sound of the Greek music Nick liked to have on during sex out of her head. Ugh. Dirty. It was too soon.

But Agnes was committed to seeing where this relationship would go; she just wasn't ready to be intimate...with anyone. She was very grateful that Wilson seemed sort of shy about sex. She didn't know about The Plan. That Saturday Night, Wilson came up with a Plan B. It was really just a variation of the original Plan, but it had a kickstarter. He would invite her over for a romantic dinner at his place; ply her with enough alcohol to satisfy an entire bowling alley on a league night, just to kind of give nature a slight nudge, without being pushy. He thought of it more as a nudgelette.

The plan seemed to be working. She took the bait and was guzzling down the $90 a bottle wine almost as fast he could pour. There was no, "It tastes a bit oaky, but it has a smooth finish," coming out of Agnes. She just kept raising her glass for more. As she was finishing her dessert *aperitif,* Agnes suggested they move over to the couch. Wilson rubbed his hands together, looked upward and silently said, "Thanks."

She snuggled into Wilson's open arms and began to snore with a lot more volume than her size would lead you to think she was capable of. He tried to shift positions to see if that would wake her up, but the snoring just changed pitch. Now Wilson found himself on the horns of a serious ethical dilemma. He could just put a blanket over her here on the living room couch and go to sleep alone in his bedroom. But that, of course, could really rumple her clothes and might make her enormously uncomfortable later. Or, he could take her clothes off, place her gently in his bed, lay down naked next to her and take his chances with whatever happened, hoping for the best.

He quickly decided that rumpling her clothes was an unacceptable outcome so he bent down to pick her up and carry her to his bedroom just in time to have her throw up all over his new Ralph Lauren sweater, bought just for tonight. As he came to find out on several other alcoholic occasions, Agnes was quite adept at saying "No" under almost any circumstance, regardless of the amount of alcohol she consumed. So Wilson decided that the best course of action for him was to go back to Plan A. The girls from the escort service never said, "No."

- Why don't we start with oral sex? Talk dirty to me.

- With you? Don't make me laugh.

- But it's a school night.

- You don't have time to hear all my reasons.

- My standards can only be lowered so far.

You Can Tell That She's Lying Cause She Looks Angry

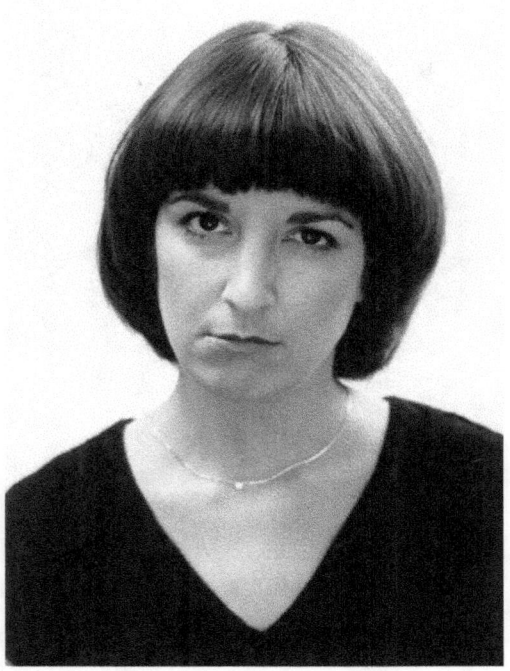

Figure 4: You can tell that she's lying because she looks angry

- Whining may work with your mother, but it won't work on me.

- Let's not, and you can tell your friends we did.

- Not even if it would save all the baby seals.

- Why do you think our *FaceBook* status is "non-existent.

Little Known Bad Sex Facts: People foolishly believed that Amelia Earhart really wanted to be the first woman to fly around the world and that's how she lost her life. Ha! She was already the first woman to fly solo across the Atlantic Ocean. So that wasn't it. She had nothing left to prove. Once she became famous, she got hit on by every man she met. Some just found her attractive, some were adrenaline junkies and some wanted to use her for her celebrity. But, they all came on to her. She got so tired of saying "no" that she ran down to the hanger with a six-pack, and with tears in her eyes, jumped into her plane, took off... and the rest is history.

- This is embarrassing. I have a yeast infection.

> ### Toolbox Tips to Control Rejection Using Metaphors
>
> Let him know artfully through the use of metaphors and similes. For example, let him know that he is looking at you as a piece of meat, and you are a vegetarian.

You Can Tell That She's Lying Cause She Looks Passive

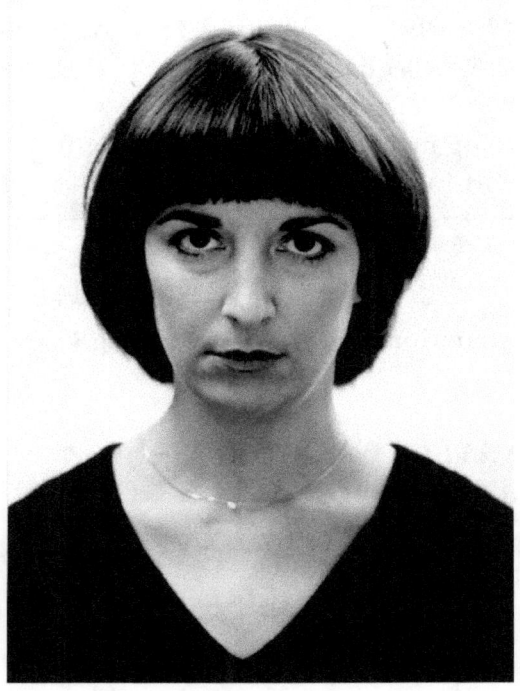

Figure 5: You can tell that she's lying because she looks passive

- I don't think you'd satisfy me.

- Wouldn't you like to tell our children we had the strength to wait until the time was right?

- When we do, I want it to be perfect. It's almost perfect.

- I'm really too good for you.

- I won't sleep with anyone who still gets an allowance.

- No!!!

The Bad Sex Manual Hall of Fame
- Not tonight... I have a headache.
- I'm on my Period.
- I'm saving myself for my wedding night.
- I'm a virgin.

Clinical Instructional Sequences: Saying No
1. Say, "No."

Thing To Avoid for Women who say, "No."
1. Avoid anything negative
2. Avoid smiling
3. Try to avoid guilt

The Case of Maggie Z.

Maggie's hero was Nancy Reagan, originator of the War on Drugs. Nancy came up with the term "Just Say NO." Maggie refused to refer to Nancy Reagan as her "heroine" just out of respect for her war. Maggie had t-shirts, sweatshirts, baseball caps and a lunch box that all said, "Just Say NO." It's a good thing she wasn't into tattoos. Over the years, Maggie found her attitudes getting narrower and she shortened her favorite phrase to "No."

She believed that refusing almost any form of pleasure made her a better person. It made her feel stronger. By her junior year in college, she finally came to terms with the fact that her favorite word and her popularity, or lack of it, might be related. She tried to change, but old habits die hard.

Treatment 1: Her therapist suggested that she try saying "Yes" to holding hands. After three tries, she totally mastered it and was ready for the next step. It was kissing. That did not go quite as well. She even tried doing it with one lip at a time, but it was very difficult. By the end of her senior year a boy had gotten to second base with Maggie, but only by saying that there was a fly that kept landing on her chest and he was trying to brush it off.

Treatment 2: Now that Maggie was out of college and working, her therapist suggested that she try ballroom dancing. Here, men would ask her to dance and she could practice saying "yes." And, they would press up against her and she could learn to adapt to the closeness at her own pace. A scant two years later, she was pretty comfortable with dancing, but no closer to third base.

Treatment 3: The therapist suggested that she try alcohol to lower her inhibitions.

Treatment 4: Her next therapist suggested that she try a grammatical/logical approach. Every time she started to say "No" she should do it twice because a double negative turns out to be a positive. Maggie is now having sex with two men at a time, but trying desperately to work back down to one.

What she can say when...
he notices how overweight she is.
(What's the big idea?)

Chapter 8A: Physical Attributes: She's Fat

Responses When He Notices She's Chubby

- All this foreplay is making me hungry.

- You keep any loose change you find in the folds.

- Don't worry, I don't like to be on top.

- I'm not overweight... I'm voluptuous.

- Is it my fault that Weight Watchers doesn't work?

- If you can stay on for more than 8 seconds, you get a rodeo belt.

- I'm a great cook.

- Freedom of expression begins with the body. It's right there in the First Amendment.

- Just think of it as more to love.

- I hope you're not the type that only likes anorexic models.

- Does a big woman intimidate you?

- Italians think that ample women are desirable.

- If you're not man enough to handle a woman my size, don't waste my time.

- I'm light on my feet.

- I learned in my photography class that the camera adds ten pounds. The male eye actually puts on thirty.

- I'm easy. I'll eat anywhere, anything…

- Underneath I'm gorgeous.

> ### Toolbox Tips to Deal with Weight – Guilt
> When he shows you his reaction to your weight, immediately break down and weep. Don't cry… weep. Shoulders should shake, breath should be tortured and sobs should abound. He will be so consumed with guilt that he will be diverted from what he saw. This works best with Catholic and Jewish men.

- My ex-husband tried to keep me fat so I wouldn't look attractive to other men.

- I also have a large appetite for sensuality.

- It's just water retention.

- With all the starving children in the world, I feel guilty to leave any food on my plate.

Teaching Stories
Coffee With Sally

As far as anyone could remember, Sally hated to exercise. As a kid, when her mom told her to go out and play she grabbed a doll or two and did the same thing outside as she did inside. Throughout her school years she was a virtuoso at inventing reasons to get out of gym class. Exercise was smelly and dirty. Sally liked nice girlie things.

It shouldn't come as a surprise that Sally's sustained inertia led to a few unwanted pounds each year. Nothing drastic, just a slow gentle ascent. In high school she was described as *plump*. In college she liked to think of herself as *robust*. And now at the age of twenty-nine, trundling downhill toward thirty, she tried not to describe herself at all.

Sally was surrounded by a caring group of friends, both male and female. Given the frequency of Sally's romantic encounters (none), there was growing consensus that Sally needed a date, and soon. But Sally had almost as many excuses to keep from going on blind dates as she had excuses to get out of P.E. Most gave up trying to set her up. That's when Adele, Sally's best friend, decided that in Sally's best interest, she had to "get up in her grill."

Adele knew Sally intimately enough to spot all the lies Sally manufactured to protect herself. In the middle of yet another excuse, she just interrupted her and said, "Sally, it's O.K. to be scared. But you know, 'no pain … no gain.' " Adele immediately cursed herself for using the word "gain," but she kept pushing forward. "What are you afraid of?"

Through the tears falling into her mac-and-cheese Sally said, "What happens if he doesn't see my inner beauty because of all this?"

Adele tried to comfort her with, "Then he doesn't deserve you and we'll find you someone else … someone better. Come on, it might even be fun. We'll get your hair and nails done, go shopping for some new clothes, it'll be a blast."

A reluctant Sally said she would try, but she swore Adele to secrecy. She said it won't be a blind date because no matter how discreet everyone promised to be, her entire social network would eventually find out all the details. She promised she would do it on her own.

A shaken Sally managed to make it home and was certain she had just made a deal with the devil. How was she going to find someone to go out with? She had no chance in a bar or pick-up spot. She decided that she would cloak herself in the anonymity of the Internet. She went with *match.com*. She took a few dozen selfies and then, using *PhotoShop,* made just a few miniscule changes until she liked the girl in the photo who was looking back at her.

Then it was time to write a profile. Should she mention the meager 50 or 60 pounds she was thinking about losing? Probably not because she still had a few weeks to work on that. Of course a gym was out of the question, but there was dieting, and lots of pills on the market and let's not forget praying for the Lord to help her.

So she wrote her profile highlighting that she loved to travel, liked to cuddle in front of the fireplace, watch foreign films (not movies) and take long moonlight walks on the beach. Her hands shook as she read the phrase "long walks." She hated any kind of walking, but after reading a bunch of other female profiles, it seemed to be a requirement. Then she posted her photo and profile and sat exhausted. As she was drinking a tall diet Coke she said, "Yes, I've just started my diet."

After a load of laundry, she came back to twelve messages on *match.com*. She shouldn't have been so surprised because she did have a pretty face, especially after *PhotoShop* helped reduce the horizontal perspective of the photo by 16%. Now she had to start combing through the guys who had contacted her. When she thought about being with them she was surprised to find herself starting to enjoy the process, but then she thought about them seeing her and cringed.

By this time there were 37 men who responded to her post. She ruled out 29 of them for a variety of reasons and ranked the 18 who were left on a 1-to-10 scale. Instead of starting with the 10s, she opted to start with Paul, the lowest ranking guy...a shaky 6.

Paul
Paul was a forensic accountant, whatever that was. He was 34 years old, divorced for six years with no kids. He wore horn-rimmed glasses and was sort of ugly in an interesting way. He liked jazz, animals, going to small theaters and reading. He didn't mention long walks so he seemed fairly safe to Sally. Sally liked the fact that he was divorced. He already had any delusions about perfect relationships and soul-mates beaten out of him. He was coming in "pre-bitter." He was 5'6" which was on the short side so he has already tasted the fruits of negative physical evaluation and self-loathing. She felt a small glimmer of hope.

They made a date for coffee at 4:45 in the afternoon on Thursday. That would give Sally six days to worry a few pounds off. During those six days she starved herself, and actually used the stairs once. Sally lived on the 2nd floor. On Thursday morning she finally jumped on the scale to discover that she had lost close to half a pound. What to do?

Thursday
On Thursday at 1:00 P.M. Adele came over to help Sally. She showed Adele Paul's profile and Adele said, "He's perfect for a trial run." Sally started to cry and said, "No. He's the one I want to end up with. I really like him."

Adele pointed out that they still hadn't met yet. But she didn't know that they'd been emailing and texting every day. The only things keeping them apart were that they haven't spoken to each other directly or seen each other yet. Sally began to shake. "What happens when he sees me? All of me? Oh, this was such a bad idea. Adele, what have you gotten me into?"

Adele said, "Look, if you don't want to go, don't go. We both know that you're really just afraid. I promise, no matter what happens, you'll come out a winner. If he doesn't work out, you can make the decision to try again, lose weight or switch to women." Sally laughed, unaware that Adele was now an active bisexual with stronger leanings away from the direction men daily. None of her friends knew.

Coffee
Sally was already sitting when Paul came in. And he was fifteen minutes early. They both started to laugh when they realized they were both nervously early, but only their mouths laughed. Their eyes were not involved in the laughter at all. Paul was almost the advertised 5'6", but just a touch on the minus side. To compensate, he couldn't have weighed more than 125 pounds.

Sally was sitting with a large purse against one side of her body and a huge sweater wedged in on her other side. Her dress was loose fitting with a dizzying array of colors in a futile attempt to camouflage her excess weight. If we took a scientific poll of everyone in the coffee shop, it would show that she was fooling none of them. Her first thought on seeing him was, "If I'm ever on top, I'll crush him." His first thought was, "Never let her roll over and be on top, she'll crush me."

If Sally wasn't so busy trying to cover herself, she would have noticed that Paul was wearing shoes that added an inch to his stature. Paul was too engaged in moving nonchalantly to really take in all that Sally was concealing. Coffee went well, they began dating and everyone was happy, except perhaps Adele. She was sorta' happy, but perhaps a bit disappointed.

- You obviously don't read Vogue. This year it's full figure.

- And it's all yours!

> ### Toolbox Tips to Deal with Weight – Fault Finding
> As soon as he makes a reference to your width, or even if he lingers too long with his eyes and makes a bad face, spring into action listing his flaws. Do not limit yourself to his actual flaws. You can start pointing out flaws you suspect he might have. This is a numbers game, just like your weight. A good rule of thumb is to list a flaw for each five extra pounds you are carrying. As he is forced to defend himself, you will be in the clear. He will soon begin to beg you for a second chance.

- Wait till you see me belly dance.

- I eat when I'm depressed. I've gained 25 pounds since we started dating.

- I'm as good as any two of your old girlfriends.

Little Known Bad Sex Facts: In this picture of Samson and Delilah, she not only fills out her skintight dress, but her tummy is held tight by three huge leather belts that are pulled so tight that she couldn't eat or drink in this outfit. Here's the real story about why Samson cut his hair. Delilah loved it. One morning, Samson surprised Delilah when she was bathing, saw her stomach in broad daylight and cut his hair so that she would stop hanging around him. The weakness that resulted came from lingering images of what Samson had seen that morning.

- Want to try a ménage a deux that'll feel like a trois?

- Think exotic... I'm your Harem.

- I thought you said you liked big breasts?

- I'm a victim of addictive personality.

- Making love to me is like being in the middle of an orgy.

- No sex and stay skinny, or take the pill and gain weight... your choice.

> **The Bad Sex Manual Hall of Fame**
> - It's genetic.
> - I have big bones.
> - I have a great personality.

Recommendations: Overweight
1. Avoid restaurants on dates.
2. Avoid any form of light.

Thing To Avoid for Women who are Overweight
1. Avoid see through anythings
2. Avoid small men
3. Avoid delicate men
4. Avoid restaurants
5. Avoid State Fairs
6. Avoid daytime

The Case of Florence S.

She grew up thin and not liking to eat. This is not a surprise because Florence came here with her family at the age of four. Although they all left England behind, they took its cuisine with them. Until the age of 14, Florence had only eaten her mother's cooking. She never enjoyed eating. In fact it was tortuous. Then one day on a school outing, she tasted a slice of pizza and something miraculous happened. It was like Easter and her salivary glands were resurrected. Then she ate a burrito and thought she had died and gone to Mexican heaven. McDonalds, KFC, chocolate chip cookies and other marvelous occurrences caused her thoughts about taste to grow, along with her waist size, but who cared?

By the time she graduated high school, her graduation robe was skin-tight. On graduating from college, her robe bulged, but she was happy... sort of. All of her girlfriends were going out on dates, but Florence's phone was ringless. Boys texted her friends, but she was textless. Something had to be done.

Treatment 1: Her therapist suggested that she go on a diet. She eagerly agreed, as long as she didn't have to give up eating any of the foods that she liked.

Treatment 2: The therapist then suggested that she eat a bit less, and begin an exercise program. She agreed to the exercise program. She would walk everyday for half an hour. As it happened, her favorite shopping center was a 15-minute walk from her house. A round trip was exactly 30 minutes, mission accomplished. It was perfect except for one little thing. The walking made her hungry. So when she got to the shopping center she ordered a pizza. But, she only ate a single slice, until she got home and finished the rest.

Treatment 3: She went online and found that there was a group of guys who fancied themselves as "chubby chasers." Case closed.

What she can say when...
he sees her small breasts.
(The Cup is Half Empty)

Chapter 8B: Physical Attributes: Underdeveloped

Responses When He Notices Her Small Breasts

- This let's us get a lot closer.

- They get bigger when touched by a *real* man.

- Do you want a woman or a cow?

Small Breasts – Before Camouflage

Figure 1: Pre-camouflaged Small Breasts

- They look bigger when you squint.

- They'll never sag.

- I smoked as a kid and it stunted their growth.

Small Breasts – Sweater Camouflage
Sweater   Crosses Sleeved   Sweater

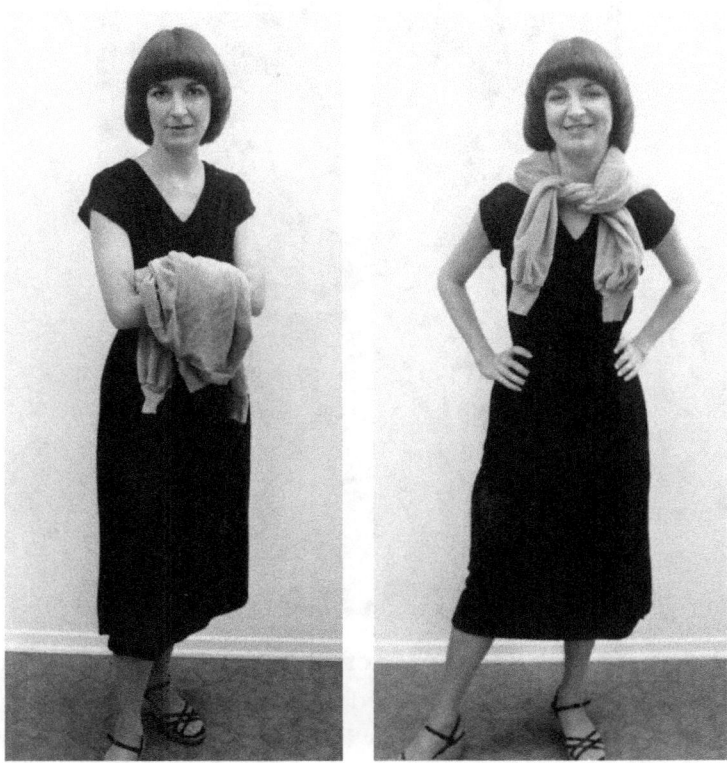

Figure 2: Camouflaged by sweaters

Little Known Bad Sex Facts: Joan of Arc was flat as a board. No men ever chased after her. So the only way for her to have men follow her around was to lead an army. It was strictly ego that caused her to have great military victories. Unfortunately for her, before she could actually get her hands on a man, the British captured her. They refused to believe that a woman could ever win a battle against them. They claimed she was a man. When she claimed to be a woman, they refused to believe her. She screamed, take off my clothes and see for yourself." They ripped off her top and decided they had seen enough and immediately had her burned at the stake.

- Aren't you titillated by sexual ambiguity.

- They're bigger than yours.

- They never get in my way.

- Men who like big breasts are subconsciously lusting after their mother. Do you really like big breasts?

Small Breasts – Container Camouflage
Glass   Mug

Figure 3: Camouflaged by containers

Teaching Stories
Size Matters (Above the Waist)

Brad was breast fed until the age of six. The only reason his mother weaned Brad off the breast was the impending arrival of his sister. She was a card-carrying member of La Leche League. If you hadn't heard of them, they are fanatical about the health benefits of breast milk and have been known to continue breast feeding into a child's early teens.

Brad was breastfed on buses, in movie theaters, while friends came over to the house to play, even in church. And Brad, who is now 36 years old, still loves breasts, particularly big ones because they look and feel more nurturing.

This has proven to be a bit of a problem over the years. It's impossible to count how any times Brad has heard the expression, "Hey, my eyes are up here." Because Brad always strived to be honest, he would answer, "Yes, they are right where they belong, but your breasts are down here."

Until he met Sharon, his fixation did not present much of a problem for his relationships because he was drawn to women with big breasts so it was never a topic of conversation. Then he met Sharon, who had read a copy of *The Bad Sex Manual* and knew how to camouflage her small breasts. They went out several times and Brad developed a huge crush on her and then the moment of truth arrived, and he was not ready for it.

Since Brad never paid attention to small-breasted women, he didn't realize that he had a problem with them. But boy did he. Unfortunately, now he was hooked on Sharon and large breasts, which she didn't have. A serious choice was looming.

He talked to some of his female friends about it. In their own supportive way they told him he was a misogynous pig. Some didn't take that much time with him and just said he was a pig. Brad remembered an old Hungarian saying, "When three people say you're drunk…you're supposed to lay down." It was time to find professional help. Brad was determined to see a therapist.

He decided that he would be more comfortable with a male therapist, but might learn more from a female therapist. He decided to see a female therapist anyway. When she heard about how he was brought up by a La Leche extremist, she was very empathic. She joked that "man can't live on milk alone," but he explained that he did for years. And he had a wonderful relationship with his mother to this day. She asked if he told his mother about his problem. He politely asked his therapist if she was crazy. As he was turning purple he said he and his mother could never talk that way to each other.

When she asked if he and Sharon were sexually active, he said they had sex a few times, but he wouldn't describe it as active. He said it was always done in the dark with her lying flat on her belly. Brad tried to make a Greek joke that his therapist explained was insensitive on a number of levels.

As their relationship got more intense, sex had become less frequent. Sharon was beginning to ask questions, and the last time they were in bed she popped the big one. Did he have a problem with her breasts? Brad said, "Hmmm…let me think about that one," and ran out the door, straight to his therapist. He was willing to pay double for an emergency session.

At this point, his therapist suggested that they try desensitization. She began by showing him cartoons with small-breasted women and followed it up with photos. She replaced the normal fully stuffed pillows on her couch with barely padded pillows and told him to try and get comfortable with them. She brought out an inflatable woman with small breasts and had Brad fondle them. Brad left in the middle of the session, vowing to find a new therapist. A male therapist this time!

They jumped right in, and he asked Brad what small breasts symbolized for him. He asked if it meant lack of nurturing, unresolved conflicts with his mother or did he just like big tits. Brad said he wasn't sure. His therapist brought out three large dolls. Each had bigger breasts than the next. Brad put the one with small breasts aside, poked the one with moderate size breasts a little, put it aside and then mashed the one with the large breasts into his face moving his head back-and-forth smiling and saying, "Mmmm."

His therapist, who had a passion for electronic gadgets, suggested that they try aversive counter-conditioning. When Brad asked what that was, the therapist said he would demonstrate. He clipped a pair of electrodes to Brad's ears, handed him the large breasted doll again and waited for Brad to begin fondling it again. As soon as he did, the therapist flicked the switch and delivered a small electric shock to Brad's ears. He was surprised to see almost no change in Brad. He turned up the level of shock until Brad finally dropped the doll and yelled, "Hey, that hurts!"

The therapist explained that they would do this every day until Brad was "cured." Those were the last words Brad heard him say. He decided on a bold course of action. He called Sharon for a date, arrived with a huge bottle of Scotch and so began a course of alcohol therapy. They both got blind drunk, and had great sex every day for the next seven months.

Pamela was the best AA sponsor they could ever have hoped for, even though she had small breasts. She was so nurturing that Brad began to feel close to her. Sharon also got attached and now the three of them are living together in Soho, and as far as Brad is concerned, their two sets of small breasts added together is close enough for him.

- What would you differently with them if they were bigger?

- In Jr. High you would have killed to rub your hand across a training bra.

- If they were much bigger, you'd be too intimidated to approach me.

- They're a perfect size for a latent homosexual fantasy.

- Touch them ... they feel way better than they look.

- You won't feel awkward unhooking my bra.

Cup Size by Occupation

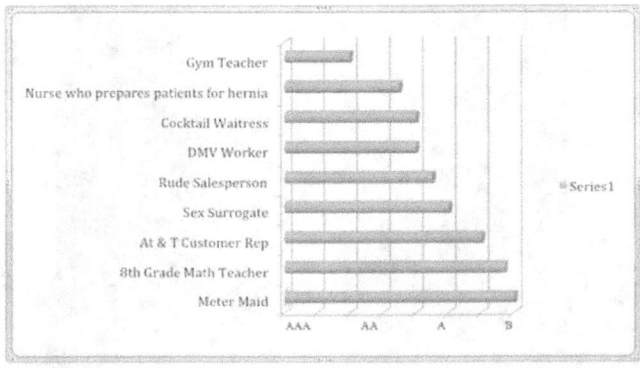

Table 2: Cup (Breast) Size by Occupation

- They were fashionable in the 1920s.

- Since they're harder to find, you'll appreciate them more when you do.

- Go on... I've heard them all:
    - Two fried eggs on a nail
    - A couple of Bulls Eyes
    - A pirate's dream... A sunken chest
    - A pair of mosquito bites

Small Breasts – Object Camouflage

Purse **Book**

Figure 4: Camouflaged by objects

- It's like going from first base right to third.

Small Breasts – Crossed Arms Camouflage

Figure 5: Camouflaged by Crossed arms

> **The Bad Sex Manual Hall of Fame**
> - I never ruin my sweaters by stretching them out.
> - They're made to fit into champagne glasses, not beer mugs.

> ### Toolbox Tips to Deal with Small Breasts
> ### Increase Size
>
> One of the most effective and satisfying ways to increase your bust size is to go on a weight gain program. The bad news is that you must also exercise a bit, but just a bit. The key is eating. Your breasts are made up primarily of fatty connective tissue. Increase your weight and two things will begin to happen (we're counting both breasts as one thing in this calculation): Your breast will grow and you will be happier because you get to eat more. You're welcome.

Clinical Instructional Sequences: Small Breasts
1. Disguise with many layers of clothing.
2. Avoid Summer.

Thing To Avoid for Women who Have Small Breasts
1. Avoid any type of melons
2. Avoid men with large hands
3. Men who like to hold hands and walk alongside you
4. Avoid tank tops, tube tops, t-shirts and blouses
5. Avoid wearing only one sweatshirt
6. Avoid men with a hostile sense of humor

The Case of Jean M.

Jean was a fast developer. Throughout elementary school, she was taller than all the kids in her class. She learned to read better and faster, she was better in math and could throw a ball farther. She was developmentally ahead by a landslide until the boys' voices started to change, everyone was growing hair in strange places and training bras started appearing in the Girls' locker room. Soon, Jean didn't want to shower with the other girls, carried her school books clutched across her chest and always wore a thick sweater.

Kids notice stuff. Comments began to fly and nicknames morphed into taunts that turned to cyberbullying. As a senior in high school, she was exposed for stuffing Kleenex into her training bra. The Internet was all atwitter. She decided to become morally loose to see if that would help, but the boys never took her seriously and joked about never being able to find "Second Base."

Treatment 1: The therapist suggested that Jean look for boys to date at college that were brighter and deeper and less interested in superficial matters. Unfortunately, the therapist, being a woman, was surprised to discover the depths of superficiality in college boys, even the smart, nerdy ones. Perhaps especially the smart, nerdy ones.

Treatment 2: The therapist suggested that Jean look into getting implants.

Treatment 3: The next therapist suggested that Jean try dating desperate, lonely, homely boys who have trouble talking to girls. He suggested that poor eyesight might also be a plus. This seems to be working because Jean is now dating her therapist who meets all the criteria he suggested. But, shhh, it's a secret. Let's hope the Licensing Board never gets wind of it.

Part Three: For Gay Couples

Introduction

Some of the research done by the authors was done through the interview format rather than through direct interaction. The information in this section was done solely through extensive interviews. We would like to point out, however, that we each have many gay friends.

Bad Gay Sex

Bad sex in the LGBT community is basically the same as in the heterosexual community except that there is a higher probability that your partner is more likely to resemble you chromosomally.[1]

---

1 *Note:* This analysis is based on large-scale, aggregated probabilistic calculations that have been normalized to represent samples that are skewed toward urban areas and tend to be weighted more heavily due to larger concentrations of our samples living in denser populations situated in coastal regions.

Part Four: Bad Sex in the Fast Lane

(Bad Kinky Sex)

Introduction

At the Clinic, we get a lot of people sending us their stories about bad sex. We were surprised to find that many of them involve what has come to be called in the parlance of the street, "Kinky" sex. In most of these instances, it doesn't turn out so well for either party. Perhaps it isn't even appropriate to use the word "party."

In the interest of providing additional material that our readers my find clinically adaptive, we have chosen to include a bit of narrative, followed by a clinical anecdote here. Each example was selected because of its instructional utility. A friend of ours referred to them as the Bad Sex version of the *Penthouse Forum*. We aren't speaking to him any longer. It is our profound hope that you benefit from these "kinky" instructional chronicles organized around the basic Bad Sex issues.

Men's Kinky Edible Sex

A long time favorite of the borderline kinky sex activities has been the use of whipped cream in the bedroom. It is typically spread across a partner's body, particularly around the erogenous zones, and then licked off. It has become a popular type of foreplay.

Premature Ejaculation – It will not surprise anyone to read that when a tongue arrives within two inches, the "problem outcome" is invoked, followed by shame and a lot of silent, awkward clean up. Typically, there is no eye contact for at least 20 minutes afterward.

> **A Case Study about Edible Sex (Premature Ejaculation)**
> Joey M. had a premature ejaculation history that predates losing his virginity by 4 years. When he was 26 years old he met Olga in his AA class. Olga was very proud of the fact that she has been sober for 8 months and has progressed to where she was just as uninhibited sexually when she is sober as she was when she is drunk.
>
> She was on her first date with Joey and during dinner, insisted that they not have dessert. She urged Joey to go back to her place for a very special dessert that she would prepare for him. This took Joey by surprise because he was so focused on trying to distract himself because Olga

had such a perfect body. He was afraid of what he knew would happen if she touched him...anywhere.

When they got to her apartment, Olga dimmed the lights, ran into the kitchen and came out shaking an aerosol whipped cream container. She sprayed a little on his lips, giggled and then licked it off. Then she asked him to take his shirt off telling him that this could get a little messy. As soon as he did, she sprayed whipped cream on each of his nipples. Then she slowly started to lick each one.

That was it. He spent himself during the middle of the second nipple lick. His present goal was to be as still as he could and just sink down into the couch. Olga was blithely unaware about what happened until she pulled down his pants and saw the mess in his underwear. At first she laughed a little, then she told him she was tired and he should leave, then she reached all the way back in the freezer to find her favorite vodka bottle. She drank several glasses without squirting any whipped cream on the glass.

Impotence – A choice of many sufferers of impotence is to combine the feel of foreplay, the sight of a naked partner and lavish sexual imagery in an effort to achieve an erection. The addition of a cold spray of whip cream does not help in any way. It makes things even worse under the following conditions:

- If he is a bit OCD about neatness, and worse still if he has just changed his sheets that day...
- If she is a bit overweight and dives in for the whip cream while salivating...
- If he is a vegan...
- If it's cold in the room...
- If she uses a spoon...

A Case Study about Edible Sex (Impotence)
The three most common causes of impotence are a proclivity toward anxiety (particularly the type brought on by shame and embarrassment), a short attention span and a poor self-image. Wilton M. displayed all three. (Please look past the play on words between his name his problem.)

Almost any social situation set Wilton's nerves on edge. Loud noises terrified him, women brought on innumerable fears and intimacy scared him to a level that wouldn't fit on any scale we tried to graph it on.

Any form of change distracted Wilton. If it got warmer or colder, it diverted his attention. If he was reading the paper and music came on, he'd lose his place. It's not a surprise that when he was with a woman, which was a surprise in itself, that her slightest movement would distract him causing a state of flaccidity that became the bane of his existence.

To evidence Wilton's self-image, he had only one small mirror in his house. It was generally kept covered. He was careful not to appear in anyone's photos. He discounted his appearance, creativity and intellect. But none of these factors contributed to his low self-concept more than living with the burden of his impotence.

He was about to have a fourth date with Rina. He met her online and thought she might be *the one*. He was terrified because they had already gotten a little beyond second base. Wilton had never talked about his problem to anyone, but this time he felt that he just had to get some outside help. He decided to confide in Michael, his closest friend. After a bout of nervous giggling, Wilton finally unloaded his problem. He was caught off-guard seeing his friend smiling. He was feeling a bit hurt until Michael explained the simile. He confessed to having a similar issue and said he was getting past it by working with a Clinical Sex Surrogate. He willingly shared her contact information.

As Michael handed Wilton her card, Michael gave him a little smile and said, "She can sometimes be a bit unorthodox in her approach." When Wilton asked what he meant by that, his friend said that he shouldn't have even mentioned it. When Wilton smiled and said, "Hey, is this a joke? Are you giving me the number of some hooker?" His friend assured him that she was a State Licensed Clinical Sex Surrogate and he could probably even deduct her services on his taxes as a legitimate medical expense.

Wilton made an appointment and arrived at her office at 3:00 P.M. on the following Thursday. He sat in the Waiting Room alone. After a few minutes she called him into a small consulting room with a desk and two comfortable chairs. She motioned for him to sit and describe his *situation*. She was very careful never to use the word "problem."

It took Wilton a few minutes to get used to talking to a fairly attractive woman openly about sex, particularly his own. She jumped right in and soon asked if he indulged in self-gratification, perhaps while viewing Internet pornography. Blushing all over, he couldn't manage to utter a response. She said that his reaction to the question was illuminating and provided a good part of the answer she was looking for. But what she really wanted to know was whether the same state of flaccidity plagued him during these sessions as opposed to when he was with a woman. He managed to shake his head back-and-forth vigorously to indicate that it didn't.

She suggested that since it was their first session, they should approach things slowly. She led him into her inner office. Wilton was shocked to see that her inner office seemed to be a bedroom with a small refrigerator in the corner. She suggested that since it was his initial visit, they only strip down to their underwear to reduce the possible tension. Wilton was afraid the top of his head would explode.

He was surprised when she poked him in the ribs to see if he was ticklish. He laughed uncomfortably, while she commented on how happy she was to see him laughing. "We don't want this to be scary, it should be fun." Then she went over to the refrigerator and pulled out a can of whipped cream and began to shake it. Then she squirted a little dab of it on his left elbow. Then to Wilton's surprise, she leaned over and licked it off.

Then she handed the can to Wilton and said, "Now it's your turn." As he was about to squirt whipped cream on his own elbow, she said, "No, silly. On *my* arm, so *you* can lick it off me." Fighting through his fears he squirted way too much on her arm so she wiped some of it onto her knee. She said, "After you lick my arm, you can lick the whipped cream off my knee."

During the next session, off came their tops and the licking continued. Within five weeks, and an ample supply of whipped cream, Wilton was able to get and maintain an erection. Over the next few weeks, they tried to generalize the treatment solution to chocolate sauce, honey and even an exotic crème brulee. Sadly, none of these worked, but at least he still had whipped cream. And it worked.

In an attempt to try it out in the real world, Wilton went on *Tinder*, a tawdry dating site, and found several opportunities to try out the new whipped cream solution. It worked! He was excited to finally call Rina and ask her out for dinner. To test the waters, for dessert, he ordered a hot fudge sundae. That's when he found out that Rina was lactose intolerant.

Saying No – As you may imagine, a man who does not intend to have sex with someone will not look favorably on the prospect of being covered in whipped cream by them ... especially down there. And don't even think of suggesting chocolate syrup.

A Case Study about Edible Sex (Saying No)
Evan K. was a 35 year-old accountant. He liked things in his life to be orderly. He hung his suits by season, and within each season, from light-to-dark. He was on a first name basis with the dry cleaner down the block because he visited twice a week. He liked his clothes fresh and clean.

Evan didn't date much. Most of the dates he was fixed up with liked to drink and then get frisky. The next thing he knew, his shirt would be untucked and she would run her fingers through his hair. He didn't spend ten minutes a day combing his hair just right only to have his date mess it up. Who has that kind of time?

Evan's friends were about to plan an intervention for their friend when one of them came up with an idea. It was summer so they all agreed to have a Guy's Night at Joe's house. And they would all get in the hot tub together and talk about guy things. Evan liked hot tubs. After all, being neat didn't make him a germ-phobe nut case. As long as he knew in advance, and prepared, he liked the idea. He especially liked the way hot tubs opened his skin pores.

They agreed to be in the tub by 8:00 P.M. and they were all punctual. Then at 8:20, they all got out of the tub telling Evan they had a little surprise for him. Out came a beautiful bikini clad girl, hired from a top-rated escort service, shaking a can of whipped cream. She proceeded to put lots of it on her mouth and gave Evan a great big kiss.

The guys were looking out the window, high-fiving each other. "YES, we did it." They were too busy to notice that every time she sprayed Evan, he splashed himself with water to clean himself off. Finally, she asked him to close his eyes, lay back and relax. When he opened his eyes, he was sprayed from head-to-toe with whipped cream. He immediately ducked under the water to get it all off. Then he sprang up, grabbed his clothes, jumped into his car cursing in whatever way accountants curse. He made a note to throw his bathing suit away and find new, cleaner friends.

Small Penis – The biggest issue here, and we use that word with caution, is that his "precious" may get lost in the whipped cream. Any talk about finding it will just make matters worse. The best way might be to apply a small amount with a pastry brush in a well-lit room.

A Case Study about Edible Sex (Small Penis)
As Brett R. slogged through puberty, he went through the gangly years where his body grew really fast, except for one part. He once told his mother he had a stomach ache so he could be sent to the doctor. He had never breathed a word of his biggest fear, but he was desperate and Dr. Smits was, after all, a doctor.

Dr. Smits was very calm and reassuring. He told Brett that he was in fine health. But that wasn't what Brett came to see him for. Finally, he said, boys your age often have one or two more growth spurts. Eat your vegetables and drink your milk and we'll talk about it again next year.

Having a small penis in elementary school doesn't mean much, but in middle school, he had to start taking public showers. He waved his towel to cover himself faster than any matador flicked a cape. He was a slow starter in dating, but eventually got himself out there. And now, he had found Robin.

He had begun dating Robin two months ago. That afternoon she suggested that she come over that night and they could get *adventurous* in bed. Brett was really turned on. Brett took an extra long shower. He put on an antiperspirant that his TV said girls would swoon over. He lit incense and even changed his sheets. Evan was ready for adventure.

Robin came in threw off her overcoat. She wore nothing under it. She kicked off her shoes, reached into her purse and pulled out a multicolored gift bag and set it on the corner of the bed. She pulled out a can of whipped cream. Shook it so he could see all of her jiggle. Then she said, "I'm going to put this all over you and then lick off every little bit. Lie back and enjoy." Then she reached back into the bag, pulled out a thimble and filled it with whipped cream as she laughed and said, "I'm going to put this all over you."

This made Brett feel a sense of shame so deep that he actually considered not having sex with her. But then, he was a man so he did have sex with her. Within a few minutes of beginning, the shame was gone. When it was all over however, his need to reassert his masculinity re-emerged so he got Robin to do the dishes.

Overweight – She had better be strong because he will fight her for the whipped cream. The best strategy for her is to tell him that it's low fat. In either case, at best, it will be a huge distraction for him. If he agrees, be attuned to requests for additional condiments like chocolate sprinkles and maraschino cherries.

A Case Study about Edible Sex (Overweight)
Mitch R. was a thoughtful man. He was a strategic thinker. Every aspect of his life was organized. Especially his meals. He planned each meal carefully calculating how much to consume. Mitch hated to leave the table hungry so he always planned to make sure that he had enough calories to eat. All 247 pounds of him.

He didn't expect to date women as smart as he was. So, he was happy if they looked good, had a good sense of humor and could cook well (Not necessarily in that order.). Mary was his current girlfriend. She called to say she was coming over tonight and after dinner he should expect things to get a bit wild.

He asked Mary what she had in mind. She said it would be a surprise. Mitch didn't like surprises. He teased, "Does it have to do with dessert?" She said it did, but she wasn't going to say anymore. When she got to Mitch's apartment, she rushed to the refrigerator and quickly hid something inside. They luxuriated over a long dinner with lots of hearty red wine. Mitch thought it was a bit casky, and didn't think the finish was smooth enough, but it did its job. When the mood seemed right, they oozed into the bedroom, slowly undressed each other and then she said, "I'm going to get the surprise now." She returned with a can of whipped cream which she instructed Mitch to squirt all over her and then to lick every bit of it off... slowly.

Afterwards, she just laid there lay moaning. Then she said, "Now it's your turn." She grabbed the whipped cream and started to squirt it all over Mitch. She got about a third of the way across his belly and heard the dreaded sputtering sound. "Oh no," she said. "This is so embarrassing. We've run out of whipped cream."

Mitch pointed to the kitchen and calmly said, "Third shelf down... toward the back. Bring them both." Her hint was enough to make the surprise she had planned obvious and Mitch was well aware of his girth. So, he bought two precautionary cans of whipped cream *just in case*. After she finished licking off all of his whipped cream, Mitch laid there in pleasure, moaning. Mary was moaning too, but her moaning was caused by consuming two and a half cans of whipped cream and the ensuing nausea.

Women's Kinky Edible Sex

Frigidity – Whipped cream will just be added to a list of distractions that leads to unresponsiveness in frigid women. A better strategy might be to place the whipped cream directly into *her* mouth during sex while you focus on pleasing her. As she is busy enjoying the eating experience, you may be able to quietly sneak through and help her to reach a rare orgasm.

A Case Study about Edible Sex (Frigidity)

Emily T. had accepted the fact that she and orgasms have separate bedrooms. They were just not in her future just as they've never been in her past. It didn't make sense to her because her lack of orgasms only happened when other people were around. After not having them with a long series of men, she experimented with women. Same result. She had much better results with the Japanese. Yes, there was both Panasonic and Sony. She even had a brief Korean dalliance with Samsung. Batteries...yes, hearts...no.

Emily was the daughter of German immigrants who didn't believe that emotions should be shown on the outside. Several of her therapists suggested that she was ashamed to let her emotions out in such an unabashed manner as a loud, screaming orgasm. That led to an experiment Emily came up with.

All of her sexual partners were her equals. They had graduate degrees, successful careers and were good-looking. They were all thoroughbreds. Looking bad in front of them was unthinkable. "What if I tried random sex with someone well below my station in life?"

She flipped a coin to decide if she should go to a seedy bar to pick up this undesirable partner, or go on Tinder and pick him electronically. She decided on Tinder because she would have more control over whom she picked. What a surprise to find someone of German extraction who craved more control?

She picked Ruben. He had a minimum wage job because he was pursuing fame as a rock n' roll drummer. She liked that he was a drummer because he would at least be energetic in bed and generally have low expectations. An added plus was that he described himself as a "freak" in bed.

Ruben came to the door dressed in Levi's and a leather vest. No shirt underneath, just the leather vest. Emily had no intention of leaving the house and being seen with Ruben so she suggested that they stay in, listen to music and drink tequila. Not surprisingly, Ruben agreed. By the sixth shot, they were making out. By the eighth shot they were stumbling into the bedroom.

As they began having sex, Emily thought that her idea was working. She was relaxed, moaning out loud and liking it. Ruben excused himself for a moment. Emily thought that he was stumbling out the door, but Ruben was stumbling toward the refrigerator. He quickly came back with a can of whipped cream. They began doing more tequila shots and instead of limes and salt, they licked whipped cream off each other after each shot. Just as she was getting close, Ruben rolled over, threw up and fell asleep.

Emily found herself covered in whipped cream next to a snoring guy who was covered with whipped cream, tequila and vomit. She pushed Ruben out the door and staggered into the bathroom. Took a quick shower. Then she decided she liked her Sony best and resolved to name it Pierre.

Refusing Sex – Once again, foreplay is difficult enough with a sex refuser. By the time you take the top off the whipped cream can, she will be out the door... unless it's her place and then you will be out the door.

A Case Study about Edible Sex (Refusing Sex)
Renée got an A in her sex education class in high school. She could name every STD and recite the probability of pregnancy from each method for preventing it. She liked the idea of sex, just not actually having it. At the tender age of 24 she was the only virgin she knew. She had fooled around a few times with boyfriends after they proved that they were serious by waiting for six months. She had found ways to pleasure them, but they never got to touch her private parts directly. There was always a sheer layer of brassiere or panty protecting her.

She turned refusing sex into an art form. She could feign headaches that would fool a polygraph. She could invent excuses that would have gotten her hired in any Writers' Room in Hollywood. She could make guys feel guilty, ashamed and selfish when they tried anything. This was all great except for the fact that she was both unhappy and curious.

She had only been with Robert for five months, but decided that it was time for a little skin above the waist. She had read that licking whipped cream off each other's bodies was a good way to relax and enjoy sexual stimulation so she invited Robert over to her house. Her house meant the basement of her parents' house, but they were out of town for the weekend.

She went down to the market and bought her sexual experiment. Robert couldn't believe that this was going to happen. Being a good Catholic boy, when she said "No" he just accepted it and believed that sometimes testicles were supposed to turn blue when you sort of had sex...kinda'.

They kissed for a long time and then she asked Robert to take off his shirt. She sprayed his chest with whipped cream and then licked it off in a way that she imagined should be sensual. Robert certainly agreed. Then came the moment of truth. He had already rubbed her breasts through her blouse and bra. Then to his and her surprise, she took off her blouse AND bra. She asked him to put a tiny dab of whipped cream on one of her nipples and then gently, but quickly, lick it off. Robert was only too happy to comply.

Eight years of sexual repression melted away in four seconds. Before she realized what was happening, she was out of her skirt and panties and spraying whipped cream down there. She grabbed Robert by the hair and screamed, "Quick...lick."

Robert was as virginal as Renée, only he was a lot more scared. He had three sisters and immediately thought, "What would happen if someone did this to one of my sisters...or my mother?" He threw on his clothes and ran out of Renée's basement. He broke up with Renée in a tearful email that night. Poor Renée never even got to refuse him.

She Does But He Doesn't – This is a win-win for her. She gets to finish and have a snack on the way. Too bad for him.

A Case Study about Edible Sex (She Does But He Doesn't)
Edna M. was proud of the fact that she had few inhibitions. When streaking was fashionable, she streaked. When cocaine was fashionable, she coked. So when Al, her current guy suggested that he come over with a can of whipped cream and they use it for sex, her only question was how soon could he get there.

Edna suggested that they outline their tattoos with it and then lick it off to get things going. She liked that idea because she had a tattoo down "there" so she knew she would have a head start on getting things going.

Al was caught off guard. He expected to her to resist a little and he would have to talk her into it. She immediately took the lead. Al was a lousy follower. It was his idea and she took over as if she did this all the time and yet he knew that she was a whipped cream virgin. Unfortunately for Al, he couldn't let go of the fact that this was his thing and now she was in charge.

He went through the motions of licking, which led to sex, but he was so preoccupied that Edna had a great time, but Al had to fake having an orgasm so that he could take a quick shower and get the hell out. Now he's combing the Internet for new ways to have sex. Since he was attending chef school, he decided to use truffles next. By the time she could figure out what to do with a truffle and how to do it, he'd be done and this time, he would be the winner.

Small Breasts – This is probably the best scenario for whipped cream-based sex. The key here is to put mounds of whipped cream on her breasts and then immediately hand her an iphone so she can take a selfies. Immediately send the photo to the printer where you'll blow it up and print it out. Have her look at it while you're having sex.

A Case Study about Edible Sex (Small Breasts)
Samantha P. always dreaded the part of lovemaking that involved slowly taking off each others' clothes. She was fine once it got below the waist, but the "sweater-and-bra" stage was pure agony. It was the same with each guy. They were always polite, but seemed to let out an involuntary gasp at the sight of, or should we say the lack of sight of her tiny breasts.

Squeezing her elbows together to simulate cleavage was an exercise in futility. Dimming the lights wasn't much better. You would think that doing it in the dark would be a better idea, but it was worse. He would just keep feeling around and sometimes she could even here a whisper, "They must be around here somewhere."

A friend suggested covering them in whipped cream and getting him to lick it off. It was sensual. They could drink a little so that his perception wouldn't be quite as keen. And between the sensual pleasure of licking whipped cream while hearing the sound of a woman moaning... it just might work.

That night, Samantha said, "Let's try something new. Let's both undress ourselves and then you lay down and close your eyes until I tell you to open them." Samantha took out her can of whipped cream, dimmed the lights and used all of her sculpting skills to create a whipped cream dream of the size and shape of a set of breasts that would make Hugh Heffner drool if his body had any saliva left.

When her partner opened his eyes, his breath stopped. His tongue was already engaged in licking before his mouth opened. Unfortunately, in his excited state, it took him only a few seconds to lick off all that whipped cream. Then he uttered the words that quickly ended the relationship. He cursed the improv class that he was taking. They kept insisting that you go with your first reaction. He yelled out, "Where's the beef?"

Overweight – You will place whipped cream in all the right places and then you will have to fight her for it. This will kill the mood for sex and by the time you are both done, you will be too full to have it anyway.

A Case Study about Edible Sex (Overweight)
Ramona Q. was worried all week after her new boyfriend Bill suggested that they try licking whipped cream off each other's bodies. He had read about it in *Men's Health* magazine as a way to spice things up in the bedroom. All Ramona could think about was how embarrassing it would be if they ran out of whipped cream in the middle because of her weight.

Being a problem solver, Ramona came up with a great idea. She had a professional size electric mixer. She could make sure that they had enough by saying she liked the idea so much, she would make fresh whipped cream for the occasion. She started at 4 PM and by 7:15 she had enough whipped cream for a Roman orgy.

She decided to surprise Bill by covering herself is a thick layer of whipped cream. As Bill walked into the room, she yelled, "Start licking and you'll soon hit pay dirt." Bill started licking. Then he licked some more...and more. Within 20 minutes he ran into the bathroom and began throwing up. When he went home that evening, he immediately went online and cancelled his subscription to *Men's Health* magazine.

Men's Spanking

Premature Ejaculation – Although it's usually men who spank women, in this era of equal rights, women also spank men. Spanking is a great cure for premature ejaculation. Unfortunately, that's because it generally causes impotence.

> **A Case Study about Spanking (Premature Ejaculation)**
> John T. was 32 years old and had sex twelve times. Three of those he did not pay for. He was terrified of women and read as much as he could to desensitize himself. The reading only sensitized him more. He was on a new jag reading about BDSM and decided that if he could spank a woman, he might feel more masterful with her and that might reduce his fear of her.
>
> He went on Tinder and found a woman who was willing. They got naked and she lay across his lap. And that was the fatal flaw of the plan. As soon as he spanked her once and she wriggled... boom.
>
> Now he's reading books about restraint. We're not sure he sees the irony in it.

Impotence – As you just read, because men aren't used to, and don't generally like, being spanked, it is generally viewed by them as a distraction. Not a pleasant, erotic distraction, but one that is painful and unpleasant. This does not lead to increased blood flow and tumescence.

A Case Study about Spanking (Impotence)

Impotence puts pressure on men. That pressure, as men perceive it, comes from women. So now, spanking enters. We think you can see where this could turn out badly.

If the woman spanks the man, he will only get more afraid of women. If the man spanks the woman, there's a pretty good chance that there's a lot of repressed hostility stored up. This could put the woman in direct danger, and for the man eventually, law enforcement may become involved as well. With this little bit of a prologue...

Harvey T. was just leaving the fifth Erectile Dysfunction support group meeting this month. All told, he'd been attending these meetings for the past six months. He was very proud of the first night when he stood up and introduced himself by saying, "Hi, my name is Harvey and I suffer erectile dysfunction." After that one jolting experience, he gained nothing further from these meetings. One night, he got a bit of a thrill again by inserting the word "impotent" in an introduction instead of saying ED, but it wasn't really that much of a thrill. Maybe we can agree to call it a "thrillette."

Now that he was in every database having to do with sexual dysfunction, Harvey read about a group called "Partners with Empathy." It was a group of sexual partners whose partners didn't perform well, but they were supportive about it. Really, that's how they described themselves online. During the next meeting, they were celebrating their third anniversary with a big party, and urged all of their members, friends, guests and curious others to attend.

There were five people in the room when Harvey walked into the room. He figured he must have arrived early so he checked his watch. The meeting began 26 minutes ago and this was the entire turnout. Harvey checked out the room and saw four people who would even inspire pity from an insurance adjuster. It was sad to think about the kinds of social lives they must have, yet curiously, they were all smiling and animated. And then there was Anita. Harvey walked over to her and asked if she was in the right room.

She said, "Oh sure." These are very special people. I'm told they were a lot more attractive when they started, but apparently, being nice about bad sex has a price one has to pay. This is only my third meeting." Harvey and Anita had their first date that Friday night.

They went through the motions of dinner and the theater because they both knew why they were going out. It's a shame because Harvey's brother had written and directed the play which he ignored totally. After dinner they didn't even order dessert. They couldn't wait to get into bed together. Harvey was excited. He thought, "Hmm, maybe with a nice, empathic woman, I might not be so tense and just maybe...?"

For her part, Anita was thinking, "This is my second attempt at being nice about bad sex. It didn't work out so well with that premature ejaculator last weekend, but he was a jerk for blaming me. I thought it was a spider so I jumped just a little. And the next thing I know, he's screaming that his prematurity was my fault. Whoa Anita, let's get back to this guy and how you're going to handle it."

They undressed and the foreplay was quick. There were a few minor stirrings, and then the inevitable happened. They both just stared at its sagging form. Anita was about to show off her new empathy approach. So she said, "Listen Harvey, don't feel bad because..." Then she jumped up and said, "This is ridiculous. It's not the way we handle things like this in Oklahoma." She leaned across Harvey's lap and with raised buttocks she yelled, "Spank me Harv, and let's get this show on the road."

Harvey was no expert on empathy, but he knew this was way South of it. But, Harvey was a team player. He playfully hit Anita's buttocks with a few playful smacks. Anita screamed for him to do it *way* harder. So he hit her harder. Anita jumped up and slapped Harvey across the face leaving a red handprint. She yelled, "Get it Harvey? Harder!"

They executed this series three more times. Finally, Harvey pushed Anita off the bed and yelled, "You're nuts girl. Put your clothes on and get the Hell out of here before I call the cops." Anita quickly threw on her clothes and stormed out of Harvey's apartment. She could be heard on the staircase yelling, "What a wuss. I'm going back to Tulsa!" Harvey sat back and thought, "I guess that's enough dating for a while."

Saying No – If you spank your partner hard enough, you won't have to refuse sex with her. The problem is determining her pain threshold so that you know it is hard enough to send her packing. Unfortunately, this may cross the line into assault and battery and nothing makes sex as unpleasant as bringing an attorney into it, unless he's the one you're spanking.

A Case Study about Spanking (Saying No)
James T. has a black belt in karate, played high school football and works out at least six times a week. On some days, he does a double workout. As much as he welcomes intense physical contact, that's how much he dislikes

emotional intimacy. There are Brinks trucks that are not as armored as he is.

James is successful in business and looks at it as another form of competition. Even at work, James likes to play hard and he relishes winning in almost any form. He savors hard contact. This has lead to problems with women. He takes great pleasure in physical intensity during intimate moments in the bedroom. He is very selective about the women he lets into his life. From the moment he met Christa, he saw the red flags and knew there would be problems. But he was a man and when it comes to sex, they are colorblind.

Christa first sat across the conference room table from James and immediately applied pressure in their negotiation, serious pressure. This was complicated by the fact that she was very pretty and while pushing James in business, was coming on to him with equal intensity.

James made it a point to avoid mixing pleasure with business pleasure. He liked the competition in the office, but found himself thrown off balance by her emotional intensity. To complicate things a bit more, there was a lot he didn't know about Christa.

Christa M. grew up in a family where there was never any form of physical discipline. Her parents didn't believe in corporal punishment. She was never shaken, slapped, pinched and certainly never spanked by her parents. Being an only child she also escaped the physical abuse that so often emanates from Siblings.

During a particularly difficult negotiation, James went into the supply room for some printer paper. Christa followed him in, locked the door and simultaneously kissed

James while her hand made a grab six inches south of his belt. James was caught off-guard. The one time Christa asked James out to dinner, he had no problem graciously refusing, but engorgement clouded his thinking and they were soon petting and groping furiously.

The next thing Christa knew, they pushed the staplers, pencils and index cards off the stool in the supply room and her stomach was straddling James' groin as he positioned her across his lap, and she was being spanked. She was so shocked that she couldn't speak which means that she couldn't tell him to stop. James took this as a sign of affirmation so he continued and added a bit more vigor with each blow. As the gift of speech was slowly returning to Christa, so was the gift of thought.

Her initial reaction was fury, replaced quickly by the recognition of pain, which was slowly morphing into a weird pleasure. The only sound that came out of Christa's throat was a low gurgling, "more." After a few more spanks, she was convulsing in the agony of pleasure. Then James gently took her by the hand, guided her back to the conference room where he negotiated her pants off without ever touching them. Just as she was coming back to her senses, she saw that the deal was closed. James had successfully negotiated the deal he wanted and was leaving the room. He closed the door behind him, clapped his hands together one loud time and said, "Not that's how you say NO to sex."

Small Penis – Men with small penises generally view spanking as feedback that their penises are too small. Even when it arouses them, they are too ashamed to continue. On the other hand, if you yell, "Ouch" as they enter you, this provides a great enhancement for them. Unless, of course, you yell, "Ouch" sarcastically. They can tell.

A Case Study about Spanking (Small Penis)
Ritchie W. was a case study in "a little learning is a dangerous thing." Since middle school, when he took his first group shower in a locker room was acutely aware of his problem, or as he preferred to say, "his deficiency." He was addicted to reading psychology books. His one semester of community college didn't really prepare him for reading real psychology textbooks, so he was limited to pop psychology books. Fortunately, that is not a limitation in numbers because there are thousands of them, each with worse information than the next.

Naturally, he gravitated toward any book that mentioned the word "penis." He had recently read a new theory that reaffirmed the existence of Penis Envy and extended it to suggest two controversial theorems: (1) Men with small penises had a form of Penis Envy; and, (2) Women felt gender superiority over men who had small penises. It was like a case of "Reverse Penis Envy." It wasn't fair. He didn't get to feel superior to anyone.

When it came to dating, Ritchie only dated very short, slight women. He particularly went after anorexic women. He hoped that his size wouldn't be as much of an issue with them. Unfortunately, even these women had enough experience with other men to realize his deficiency in the dimension department.

As he got to the last chapter of the book, the author put forth another revolutionary idea. The more masculine your actions were, the less size would be an issue. The author's major contribution was that hard spanking would make the small penis owner appear more masculine and the harder the spanking, the more macho he would appear.

Ritchie never used the word "macho" because it just shined a light on what he wasn't. He brightened at this prospect. He had been hanging around an anorexia clinic trying to pick up women and found a date for Sunday night. That gave him three days to prepare. He went to the gym every day and lifted. He felt like he was in the best shape of his life, which unfortunately, was true.

He and Glory, her name was Gloria but shortening it to Glory made her feel lighter, ate at a trendy salad bar. They went back to Ritchie's apartment where he suggested that they smoke a little weed because it had no calories. Glory agreed.

Soon they were in a state of semi-undress and with no warning whatsoever, Ritchie smacked Glory's buttocks. She screamed out in pain, but was drowned out by Ritchie's scream of pain. He expected soft buttock flesh and felt solid bone. She grabbed her clothes and left cursing Ritchie. Ritchie wrote a damning response to the book on Yelp and decided it was time to take another community college course.

Overweight – The most awkward part of spanking an overweight man is the sound. It can be deafening. Make sure you don't cup your hand or it will be even louder. The other danger is that the spanking may surprise him and he may roll over on you.

A Case Study about Spanking (Overweight)
Donald J. grew up with the idea that when you want to show someone you love them, you give them food. One look at Donald tells you that a lot of people love him a lot.

When Donald made love with a woman, food was usually involved whether it was licked off the body or a snack intermission during a long love making session. If there was love, then there should be food. When Donald met Sonia, he believed he'd found his soulmate. She was a plus sized model. He thought she was perfect.

When they took their relationship to the bedroom, it became even perfecter. She was also a licker and eater. Heaven. But one night, she seemed listless during love-making and Donald asked what was the matter. Sonia said she wanted to try to get more adventurous in bed. She suggested the introduction of mild pain as a stimulus.

To Donald, mild pain was enduring a bland salad dressing so he was a bit shocked at what followed. As they were slowly undressing as part of their routine foreplay, she reached for a turkey drumstick, but instead of eating it, she hit Donald across the thigh with it. She laughed and said, "Sweets for the sweet and thighs for the thighs." Instead of thinking this was funny, Donald thought it was a waste of one of his favorite parts of the turkey (The rest of the turkey being his other favorite part). As a reflexive part of his upbringing for wasting food, he slapped Sonia across the face.

Sonia smiled, grabbed the other drumstick and hit Donald five quick times as if she was playing the drums. This caused Donald to hit Sonia back even harder. She got really turned on and gave Donald the best sex he'd had for a while and afterwards they ate a hardy meal.

Donald lay in bed trying to sort things out. He came up with a great idea. They would have sex before they ate so that Sonia wouldn't waste as much food, and from time-to-time he would smack her around if she did waste any.

Women's Spanking

Frigidity – Spanking a frigid woman can be tricky. If you do it too softly thinking that you're being erotic, it might have no effect. If you do it too hard, you will kill any chance of sexual excitement she may be about to have. If you do it just right, wow! The odds of doing it just right are 0.019 out of 1000. See, this improves your odds.

A Case Study about Spanking (Frigidity)
Marsha M. didn't think of herself as frigid. She was emotionally self-contained. No prince from Nigeria was ever going to receive a dime from her on the Internet and she never made a purchase when they advertised that she should hurry because there was a "limited supply."

She enjoyed dating and even enjoyed having sex, up to a point. She thought there was too much pressure on women to have orgasms. She didn't go in for fads. Although Marsha was generally content with her life, from time-to-time she would hear friends wax poetically about how they measured their most recent orgasms on the Richter scale.

Eventually, curiosity got the better of her. She decided to visit a therapist recommended by several of her previously non-orgasmic friends. During the first session, the therapist pointed out that in common parlance, Marsha was a "control freak" of the first magnitude. She suggested an interesting experiment. She should go to a dating site and select a nice man, but one who she perceived as being "beneath" her and let him take total control. To highlight the contrast, she should persuade him to slap her during sex causing mild pain.

She was surprised to discover just how excited she was as she went on match.com and selected Henry. He worked as an actuary at a large insurance company. He was OK looking, but clearly not up to Marsha's typical standard. Her estimate of his income was that, at best, he earned a third of what she did (not even when adjusted for gender inequity in pay). He graduated from a non-elite college. He seemed perfect, at least by her therapist's guidelines.

Henry couldn't believe his luck. He took an extra long shower before his date, bought a new dress shirt and wrote out several conversation topics so he wouldn't fold under pressure. He called several close friends and asked for their advice. They all said they have never been in this situation themselves and suggested that he should just follow her lead to avoid mistakes. When they watched football, the commentators always said that the team that makes the most mistakes will lose. It seemed like a reasonable strategy.

Henry got to the door, took one look at Marsha and briefly lost the ability to speak. She asked him in, he looked around her apartment and briefly lost the ability to breathe. He finally remembered how to breathe and talk and they chatted for a few minutes. He couldn't remember a thing that was on his list of conversation topics.

Finally, he played his strong card and asked what she'd like to do this evening. Following her therapist's counsel, she came back with, "Anything you'd like to do. I'm in your hands."

Henry froze. This wasn't what she was supposed to say. He wasn't prepared to do "any thing he wanted to do." He tried to recover with, "No really, I'm up for anything *you'd* like to do." Marsha was a bit disappointed. This was a harder assignment than she anticipated. She countered with, "No, I insist. You decide."

Henry came up with what he thought was a brilliant strategic move. He said, "Are you hungry?" Marsha came back with, "I could eat now if you'd like to go out for dinner." Henry was going down fast. Now he had to decide if they would eat or not, and if so, where to go."

Throwing caution to the wind, he suggested a trendy, but expensive Northern Italian restaurant nearby that he heard one of his bosses talk about. Marsha smiled and said that sounded great. Inside, she said, "Well, so far I have totally succeeded in lowering my standards. This restaurant will just punctuate it."

After three glasses of Chianti, Henry's speech was almost back to fluency. Marsha, in a perverse way, was beginning to enjoy the evening. She realized that Henry was very nice and having the date of a lifetime, and her date was close to actually beginning. On walking out of the restaurant, Henry was stunned when Marsha took his hand and said she'd love to see his apartment.

For most men, an unscheduled female visit to their apartment would be tragic, but since Henry was in the Accounting Arts, he always had his place in orderly shape. As his heart began beating again, he managed to nod his head in assent. As they passed a Korean green grocer, Marsha suggested that get a bottle of Chianti to preserve their mood.

They got to his apartment, found the corkscrew and half a bottle later were in the bedroom demi-naked. As they were about to have intercourse, Marsh said, "Henry, would you hit me please?" Henry was in a Chianti-induced state of confusion. For the first time that evening, Henry stood up for himself and flatly refused. He said, "I don't believe in hitting people, and I would certainly never hit a woman!"

Marsha smiled a little and said, "So Henry, you're an actuary. Do you believe in Astrology?" Henry got serious and said that Astrology was just a form of superstition and actuarial science was firmly grounded in probability theory. Marsha said, "No it isn't. Astrology gives more accurate results than insurance tables and so does a Ouija Board...and Tarot cards are more accurate too." Before Henry realized what he was doing, he gritted his teeth and was spanking Marsha the way his father used to spank him when he said something stupid.

The sex was no better than the restaurant. She felt a bit guilty about using Henry, but knew that she had given him six months of stories he could tell at the office. She made up her mind to find a new therapist who would suggest a course of therapy that involved trip to Tahiti with a wealthy, good-looking young man who reminded her of her father.

Refusing Sex – Spanking a man who you don't intend to have sex with is easily misinterpreted. We would suggest just saying "No." If you insist on spanking him anyway, here are just a few possible misinterpretations that could arise:

- If he has serious "Mommy" issues, he may follow you around forever.

- If he views you as a man-hating, castrating bitch, he my punch you.
- If you hit him just right, he will misinterpret it as a more intense version of foreplay.

A Case Study about Spanking (Refusing Sex)
Jane A. was looking for a man, but not just any man. She had a list of traits that were non-negotiable. They were carefully plotted in a spreadsheet on her laptop. So far, she hadn't met any of the three men on the planet who met all of her criteria. But that hasn't stopped Jane from looking. She was an optimist.

One criterion was that he had to be artistic. Every Monday night, which was "Gallery Night" downtown, she systematically marched through the A-list art galleries trolling for "him." She also made random visits to the three best museums in the city.

She was disturbed by the trend of diminishing bookstores because another criterion was that he had to be well-read and on Wednesday nights, she traversed her trail of new and trendy used bookstores. She also made regular visits to hear the philharmonic and top jazz acts, the best foreign and occasionally, American films, but never any movies.

She also looked at online dating. She went to great pains to write the perfect dating profile and placed so many restrictions on her search criteria that there was rarely a new entry that was even close to popping up, but she kept doggedly trying.

Jane had a phrase to describe her dating strategy, "Lots of first dates and very few second ones." Because of this, friends actually fixed her up, even though they knew it would come to nothing. Jane's friends adored her, and she was a great source of amusement to them whenever the subject of men or dating arose.

Jane had slept with two men in her life. One was the result of a drunken evening in graduate school and the other occurred on a rare third date and once again, a large quantity of alcohol was involved. Because Jane was gorgeous, she had many opportunities to turn away men's sexual advances and prided herself on her deftness in this area.

Tonight she going on a rare second date. He was clearly missing several key traits on her list so Jane knew that this one would go nowhere, but once in a while, it was fun just to have a date.

Jim was a Princeton graduate and the youngest lawyer to make partner in a prestigious law firm. He did fit quite a few criteria on her list, but unfortunately, he was also deficient on other key areas. One of the areas in which he was not deficient was networking skills. He had managed to find out the name of Jane's second sexual partner. They had an illuminating chat and Jim found out that the path to bedding her ran through alcohol. He also received some key tips about getting her to imbibe sufficiently.

Armed with this knowledge, he took her to a professional basketball game. Sport involvement was also on Jane's list. They were having a lot of fun, and chugging a few beers as the game progressed. He seemed fun and harmless. After the game, they were starving and he suggested a fantastic Indian restaurant that served very spicy food. She failed to ask the question, "What happens when you eat spicy food?" The answer is that is *you drink*. She did. They ordered a few more beers as dinner went on, and once her inhibition threshold was lowered just a touch, he mentioned a fantastic ethnic drink, omitting to mention its alcohol content.

It all seemed very innocent. She felt very safe with him, and just in case, her apartment was just around the corner if she needed to escape in a hurry. She didn't remember inviting him in, but remembered that they were laughing a lot. Before she could say, "You're missing several key criteria, her bra was off and she was laughing about it as they kissed and groped each other. Then she remembered hearing the word "interesting," and the next thing she knew, he was spanking her.

The spanking snapped her back to reality by the third slap. She just stared at him in disbelief. All at once, she realized that she had made a horrible mistake. "Oh no." She had left spanking off her criterion list. She is going out with Jim again tomorrow night.

She Does But He Doesn't – Spanking him will guarantee that he won't now, and may never again with you. If you spank him and he reacts badly, pretend that you slipped and make sure you say, "Oops" right away.

A Case Study about Spanking (She Does But He Doesn't)
For Margaret A. the difference between lust and love was just three insignificant letters. She was young enough to have a good time and wasn't going to waste this epic time in her life.

Her choice of sexual partners was capricious and varied as widely as Seattle daily weather. The only trait she cared about was that they were nice. But the meaning of "nice" could change very quickly to suit her purpose and mood.

Tonight she was out with Tony. Last week he performed at the piano lounge around the corner for four nights and performed on Margaret the other three nights. The first night was OK, but he seemed a bit less into it on the second night. Now, on the third night, there was clearly something missing. It was time for Margaret to change things up a bit.

She had been doing some serious technical reading about fulfilling sexual desires when interests begin to wane and what *Cosmopolitan* suggested was to introduce mild spanking.

That night after their first bout of intercourse, she noticed that she did, but he didn't. She leaned over and purred the following words into Tony's ear, "Baby, why don't you smack me on the bottom a few times?" Tony sat up bold upright in bed and said, "Hey Italian men don't hit chicks. We respect broads too much to do that."

Being adaptive, Margaret leaned over and said, "OK, then I'll spank you." And then she began hitting Tony playfully. As he jumped in surprise, she began to spank him harder. Soon she was doing it quite vigorously. Apparently, she was letting out her frustration over the fact that he "didn't" with her.

At that point, she discovered that Italian men had a threshold for being hit and once it was reached, their position on not hitting broads relaxed a bit. Responding more on instinct and remembering the house he grew up in, he popped her in the jaw and stormed out. Margaret made a note to write a letter to Cosmo.

Small Breasts – The smallest problem with spanking a partner with small breasts is the low probability of spanking her breasts. The biggest problem is that she might misunderstand and think you were just rough housing with her as if she was one of the boys. In this case, it would be traumatic for her.

A Case Study about Spanking (Small Breasts)
Janie Y. was very popular until middle school. Both boys and girls thought she was cute, cool and interesting and wanted to be her friend. In middle school, Janie's intellect grew, her musical talent grew, in fact everything grew, but them. Just hearing the word "pancake" could plunge her into a mild depression.

Even when kids didn't openly tease her, she knew she was a major object of derision whenever more than three kids were talking. Slowly she was demoted from the cool kids' table all the way down to the geek table. Kids are not so nice in middle school. Unlike Las Vegas, things that happen in middle school don't stay in middle school. Her chest, or her lack of one, was a constant albatross hanging around her neck because there was nothing else hanging down there.

In high school she was in the physics club, the debate team and a "mathlete." She wouldn't join the chess club because it was too close to the word "chest." In her mind, she was still a cool kid so she didn't make really friends among the other geeky kids, but her old "preflat" friends acted like they didn't know her.

She's now a junior in college. She is into "ink" and has several benign piercings and is into indie rock. Her clothes are extreme, her hair is extreme, but her lifestyle isn't so extreme. Other kids who looked like her accepted her, but she didn't accept their lifestyle so she was outwardly extreme and inwardly a poser.

She had a few careful experiments with recreational drugs, but you wouldn't call her a "druggie." She had a few poor sexual experiences and was just as self-conscious about her small breasts with extreme guys as any other guys. As a junior in college now, she decided that her best chance for romance was by cultivating her extreme lifestyle and she decided to commit more to it.

She got a few more piercings and a little more ink. That night she was going out with a guy whose name was Morris, but everyone called him "Dango" which he said was short for "dangerous." Morris wasn't a big fan of spelling. But if Morris was a Boy Scout he would have several merit badges for kinky sex and Janie was trying to psychologically prepare herself for whatever was to happen tonight.

But what happened was the last thing she expected. They got undressed and as he saw her chest he started to point and giggle. Before Janie could respond verbally, she found herself slapping Dango across the thigh because that was the only part of him that she could reach. She would have preferred his face, but sometimes you can't be too choosey.

As soon as Dango felt the pain across his thigh, he yelled, "Cool, so you like the rough stuff," and he launched a slap across Janie's thighs. They continued this way for about thirty seconds when Janie finally screamed, "Stop it! This isn't sexy. I slapped you because I hated you for laughing at me. Get out!"

Well, this was a night for surprises for Janie. Dango, who had turned back into Morris said, "Wait! You don't understand. Seeing your breasts made me incredibly happy. Take a look at this." With that, Morris pulled down his underwear to reveal one of the smallest penises Janie had ever seen. It's not that she had seen all that many, but she knew this one was really small.

She didn't laugh, out of politeness, on the outside, but inside she was cracking up. Morris said, "Don't you get it? I laughed because we are perfect for each other." They are still dating. They have transitioned back to nerdy clothing. "Dango" died that night leaving only Morris. They never spanked each other again.

Overweight – You first have to make sure that you are strong enough to spank an oversize woman hard enough to get the effect you are looking for. Then, you have to worry about startling her because she may suddenly roll over on top of you.

A Case Study about Spanking (Overweight)
Marion T. was spanked as a child. But that didn't get in the way of knowing that her parents loved her a lot. She was raised by classic "carrot and stick" parents. When she was good, she was rewarded with food, which explains her enormous size, and when she was bad, she was spanked which explains why spanking plays such a huge role in her sexual life.

Given her size, Marion was pretty well adjusted. She had lots of friends, went to lots of parties and frequently indulged in sex. She accepted her place in life and was rather fond of the "Chubby Chasers" that made up the bulk of her sexual partners. She got to do what she wanted most of the time and never let other people tell her how to live … until the intervention.

One Sunday afternoon, she walked into her apartment and was surrounded by her parents, two sisters and 27 of her closest friends. As if that wasn't enough, Dr. Bernstein, her internist, was there also. It started out very nicely. Lots of people got up to share their feelings. They all cried as they talked, and everyone in the room cried as they listened... except Marion.

She let them all have their say, thanked them for their caring, promised to change and asked them to leave and let her reflect on everything that had happened. She was happy that she was so cared about. And she had every intention of changing because she had a date with Hank in an hour. She was definitely going to change, and shower too. They were going to her favorite all-you-can-eat pasta bar. She knew the sex tonight was going to be long and painful (in the good way) so she wanted to carbo-load.

After eating and consuming three bottles of Chianti, they went back to Marion's apartment and were soon undressing on her King+ size bed. She told Hank that all she thought about during the intervention was getting them out of her place so she wouldn't be late for their date. But now, it was all kicking in. Maybe it was time to reflect, to change and grow. Maybe she should begin exercising and eating less. Maybe she should also eat more nutritional foods.

She talked about her family and how bad they would feel if anything happened to her. She felt a responsibility toward them. Maybe she should take a healthy cooking class? Maybe join a gym and take Zumba classes. She asked Hank what he thought.

Hank held her close, took a deep breath, and started to spank her across the butt. She started to laugh. She spanked him back a few times. They went at it for two and a half hours and never spoke of the intervention again. After sex, they went out for pizza.

Men Using Restraints

Premature Ejaculation – Premature ejaculators are always struggling to maintain control of themselves. Physically restraining them often backfires. Once they truly believe that they have lost control, any number of outcomes may occur:

- They may have severe panic attacks that can lead to biting, screaming and kicking. Do not do this if you live on the second floor of a small, thin-walled apartment.
- They may come to love having their hands tied so much that they can no longer engage in autoeroticism alone. In this case, whenever the urge arises, they will have to call a friend to bind their hands, then they will have to learn to use the mouse with their lips or nose and then call a friend to untie them when they are done. While this may sound funny to you now, better hope you're not one of the friends they keep calling for help.
- They may still have premature ejaculations and then get out of having to clean up after themselves because their hands are tied.

A Case Study about Restraints (Premature Ejaculation)
There are three things that cause Billy T. to have premature ejaculations, a woman touching his thighs, a woman touching his nipples or a woman touching him. The moment a woman puts her hand on his forearm, his

instinct is to run. So you can imagine when Sophie, his newest about-to-be-disappointed date suggested that she tie him up during sex.

Without realizing it, he started humming the old Martha and the Vandellas' Motown hit *Nowhere To Run Nowhere To Hide*. He panicked and tried to come up with reasons why she shouldn't do it. He could make up a story about how his brothers used to tie him up and it freaked him out, or that he was traumatized by never becoming a boy scout because he couldn't tie the required number of knots, but all of his stories had the odor of fabrication about them.

Then he began to think. "I've spent my whole life running from new experiences because they might shame me. Damn it, I'm going to try this. After all, what's the worst thing that can happen to me?"

That night, Sophie came over. She took out a bag and removed four red satin ropes and began tying his wrists to the bedpost. Then she tied his ankles as well. Billy was surprise that the ropes felt kind of good.

Realizing that his underwear was still on and not wanting to untie him, she found a pair of scissors and began to cut them off. She made the mistake of brushing her hand against one of his thighs and he erupted. Seeing that the evening was not going to go the way she wanted, and that he had ruined the satin ropes with his excitement. She calmly got up, got dressed and left Billy trussed to the bed. But she wasn't mad, just disappointed.

After straining against the ropes and realizing that he wasn't going to get them untied, Billy finally fell asleep, secure in the knowledge that Karina, his maid was due to clean the apartment at 9 AM tomorrow morning. Karina came in and it was difficult to figure out which one of them was more embarrassed. She spoke only Spanish and he didn't pay much attention in his 7th grade Spanish class, but by motioning toward the scissors lying on the bad next to him, he got Karina to understand that he wanted her to cut him loose. Karina complied, but unfortunately, during the cutting process, she touched his thigh.

Impotence – Since impotent men believe that they lack power in a relationship, restraining them only makes this worse. In the most extreme case we read about, a woman got so frustrated that she began tickling her partner until he wet himself. Then she got up and left without untying him. Since she used her stockings to tie him up, he will not date a woman who shows up in stockings or pantyhose.

A Case Study about Restraints (Impotence)
Walter W. was a great compensator. He was enormously insecure around women, so he got good at fooling them into thinking that he had confidence to burn. He was good enough to convince women that he did not have an impotence problem, but rather … they just weren't hot enough to arouse him. Women would leave his bed in tears apologizing and promising to start going to the gym the following morning. Then they would beg him for another chance in a few months. Of course, they never got that chance.

Walter sold high-end automobiles. That's the way he said it, but underneath it all, he was just another car salesman, which accounted for the fact that he could fool all these women so easily. He actually sold cars to a few of them who tried to get back into his good graces.

Tonight he had a date with a woman that had him a bit concerned. Concerned, but not worried. She seemed a bit too confident. Alice was not the kind of woman he usually went out with. She first fooled him when she came into the showroom and kept giggling about the fact that she didn't know much about cars. He found her insecurity intoxicating. When he asked if she would like a cup of tea or a glass of wine, he was a bit unnerved by her knowledge of wine, but made a date with her for dinner anyway.

During dinner, she made good use of her wine knowledge by getting both of them quite tipsy. As they staggered out of the cab and into her apartment they were already groping each other. Alice said she would like him to try something and tied a silk bandana across his eyes as she slowly massaged his shoulders and neck. So far, Walter liked where this was going. He felt very relaxed as she rubbed him all over. So relaxed in fact that he never noticed that she tied his hands and feet to the bed and then slowly pulled off the bandana.

She slowly removed the rest of her clothing in a sensual way and started doing some of the things that we all consider to be traditional foreplay. The wine helped relax him, but the edges of his mind began to worry because there wasn't much response south of where his belt used to sit. How would she react?

At first, she seemed to take this as a challenge and each new attempt at arousal felt pretty good, but that just served to increase his anxiety. The next thing he knew, she took out her iphone and began taking videos of his southern region from all different angles. With his hands tied, he couldn't cover up. He demanded to know what she was going to do with the videos she was taking.

She calmly explained that several of the women whose self-esteem he had shattered talked to each other and were furious. They hired Alice, who worked as a part-time private investigator and part-time escort to help get a bit of payback. Walter asked how much money it would cost him to buy the videos back. Alice just laughed and said, "You really don't understand women do you? They just want to see the video and get one more try with you in bed. And then they never want to see you again. They just want to prove that it's you not them."

Walter made a vow never to drink so much that a woman could tie him up again. Then he resigned himself to three future nights of impotent inner rage.

Saying No – If you don't intend to have sex with a woman, don't let her tie you up. That sounds simple, but partners can be very tricky. For example, "Here, hold this yarn while I unravel it." The next thing you know, you're tied up. Once you're tied up and say "No," you are in a bad negotiating position.

A Case Study about Restraints (Saying No)
Paul D. couldn't understand that the more he refused a woman the harder she tried to go after him. Don't they have any self-respect? Paul didn't understand the Principle of Scarcity. The less chance you have of obtaining something the more you want it.

Two weeks ago, he was thinking about buying a new stainless steel refrigerator. He wasn't sure that he wanted it until Ashley, the customer sales representative said, "This is the last one we have in stock. And we won't get any more in for months. Everyone wants them." Paul thrust his Visa card into the customer representative's hand before the she could wipe the smirk off her face. Yet he couldn't transfer that thought to the women he was chased by.

As Ashley was ringing up the sale, she asked Paul if he'd like to get a quick cup of coffee before he left. Being in a bit of a dither because he almost passed up on the refrigerator of his dreams, he agreed. As they sipped, she said, "You seem so nice. I'm so tired of every guy trying to hit on me. Thanks." Before Paul realized it, he was asking her out for dinner.

During dinner, Ashley said, "I think it's funny guys really want to get me drunk to get me into bed, but on the first date they think they're so smart by avoiding alcohol to get me to trust them. All they're thinking about is scoring on the second date. I'm so glad you're not like them."

Before Paul knew what was happening, they were sloshed. They barely made it into their Uber car on the way back to Ashley's house. He was so blitzed he wasn't totally sure what she was saying, but it sounded like, "Guys don't understand that I'd never agree to tie them up. The more they ask, the more I won't."

By the time Paul was trying to understand why men could possibly enjoy being tied up by a woman, he was experiencing it. Finally, for the first time with Ashley, he got to say "No." but by then, it didn't do much good. She had her way with him and then pushed him out the door.

The sad part was that he had a great evening with Ashley, tried to ask her out again and again. Each time he was rejected more soundly. After much reflection, he finally figured out what Ashley had done to him and decided to use the Principle of Scarcity on her. It didn't work.

Small Penis – There is probably no situation that is more embarrassing than having your hands tied, being undressed slowly and having your partner discover that you are not well endowed. If she has little self-control or a mean sense of humor you will be lucky to just be humiliated by her recognition and subsequent laughter. If she's mean-spirited you may end up with you and her in a selfies that she posts on *Instagram* and her *FaceBook* page.

A Case Study about Restraints (Small Penis)
Fletcher M. hated few things more than going into a sporting goods store needing a supporter and cup and being referred to the Boy's Section. Sometimes he would lie and say it was for his young nephew, but he would swear that he saw the salesman's eyes looking at his crotch and suppressing a grin.

Whenever he had a date and it came to the crucial moment where he would have to present himself in an undressed state he planned things out meticulously to avoid any embarrassment. First, the only light source was a very dim old lava lamp. Next, he made sure that there was a lot of incense burning for at least an hour before they entered the bedroom so when they finally got to see it, they saw it through a thick haze at best. It's almost redundant to say that by that time, much alcohol had already been consumed as well.

Probably the most genius thing that Fletcher did was placing a series of very small, decorative pillows all over the bed. This made him look proportionally bigger. Any trip to a store began with a search for a small pillow that he could add to his "comparison collection."

Fletcher was generally a pretty laid back guy. The people he worked with would never describe him as a control freak, but they never went into a darkened bedroom with him when they were drunk. In his pre-sex bedroom, it was clear that there were German Field Generals that didn't exert as much control as he did.

Before he left to pick up Evelyn for their first date that evening, he lit the requisite 20 sticks of incense, turned off all the lights but the lava lamp, then left. There was only one thing he didn't prepare for. His date urged that they go back to her house because she had forgotten to feed her cat. If he refused, he was a horrible monster who wanted to torture a cute, defenseless kitty, and if he went, he would risk an embarrassing exposure. It took him over an hour to resolve this conflict in his head.

The best resolution idea he could come up with was that they'd go back to her house, feed her damn cat, then go to his house. Damn! He didn't have a hungry pet at home. Not even a thirsty plant. It didn't matter anyway because they were so drunk that they barely managed to stagger back to her place. When they walked in, he freaked out. He had never been in an apartment that was so well lit.

Evelyn casually said, "I'm a visual person. I like to see everything in my life brightly." The glass of burgundy she handed him shined radiantly, adding to his state of inebriation. He decided he would go with the flow and then at the right time, make an excuse to leave. They staggered into the bedroom and were petting heavily above the waist with their tops removed. Fletcher wasn't used to drinking quite this much so between the alcohol and the added stress, he conked out for a few minutes. He awoke to discover that she had finished undressing him and had him tied to her large four poster bed and for a moment, was afraid of getting sunburned from all the light pouring into the room.

Panic ensued. To his surprise, she had set up an easel and was sketching him. More panic ensued. He looked up groggily and asked what happened. She said he was half asleep as she undressed him. She kept thinking he would wake up any second and they could continue their lovemaking, but he began snoring heavily. She lowered her eyes and made a quick decision. She said she could make love any time, but how often did she meet a man of his dimension and as an artist, she had a moral obligation to represent him...and it.

They didn't have sex, but he extracted a promise from Evelyn that his face would be obscured so that he could never be recognized from the picture. He didn't consider asking her out for a second date, but extracted a second promise. She swore to give him the name of anyone who bought the picture so he wouldn't ask her out either.

Overweight – Fat men are supposed to be jolly. Welcome to Jollywood. Be careful overweight men! Once you are tied up, you may get the equivalent of a one-woman intervention about your weight. Worse still, she may start grabbing different parts of your body and tell you that she will make you "squeal like a pig."

A Case Study about Restraints (Overweight)
Jerome T.'s earliest memory about shopping is looking through the cool kids' clothes then being re-directed to the Husky section. This depressing memory was offset by another happier memory...glazed donuts. And pancakes. And fried chicken. And...

Now at the age of 28, Jerome doesn't shop in the Husky Section anymore. He frequents the Big and Tall Shop. He can also find his size easily on the Internet so life is good. He still gets looks when he flies on coach. He takes up a seat and a half, but that's the one next to him's problem, not his. Life is good.

He meets the criterion for Jolly and has a great social network. One night he went to a big outdoor barbeque and met a hefty blond woman. She had a broad sense of humor and a broad behind. He first noticed her when she was standing behind him and he heard her loud, raspy laugh. Within a few minutes he had her corralled in the corner and they were figuratively laughing their asses off.

They agreed to go out the following night and decided to change things up and go to a Korean barbeque this time. She was from Texas where everything was big. They stuffed themselves and downed several pitchers of beer along with the side of beef they knocked off between them.

Then they went back to her place and he made an interesting discovery. She was not just from Texas, but she was a real cowgirl and spent a few years on the rodeo circuit. Her specialty was hog-tying cows. As they were both laughing uproariously, she pulled a decorative rope off the wall and said, "Run from here to there." As he took two steps, he found himself on the ground with his hands and feet trussed together by the lasso she was twirling a moment ago. She managed to get both his clothes and her cloths off in her drunken giggly stupor. For his part, it was the best sex he ever had that didn't involve pastry.

She promised to teach him how to use the rope so they could take turns, but only on nights when they went out for barbeque. Jerome told his broker to buy lots of stock in beef ranches.

Women Using Restraints

Frigidity – Frigid women, as a rule, like to be tied up because it gives them yet another excuse for not having an orgasm.

A Case Study about Restraints (Frigidity)

Allison Y. wasn't frigid. She was "orgasm deprived." She was going to call it "Orgasm Disenabled" bit that seemed a bit over the top. The deprivation was really starting to get to her. She is 28 years old and came close to having one a few times, but never quite got over the threshold. She became sexually active at sixteen and that may have had something to do with the problem.

Because sixteen year-old boys are not sexually experienced and prone to premature ejaculation, she never really had a shot at an orgasm even though she took five good shots at it that year. From seventeen to nineteen, she had a boyfriend named Lance who had a lot of great traits. Being an adept sexual partner wasn't one of them. He displayed a massive amount of trait anxiety around sex. For the first year, since he was eighteen and considered an adult, and Allison was seventeen and considered "jailbait," he had a mild panic attack whenever they had sex.

This didn't launch Allison into an orgasmic trajectory. They would sneak around to have sex. He was always looking over both their shoulders to see if anyone could see them. He kept Allison on the lookout as well. Anxiety can be contagious and when it came to having sex, Allison caught a massive does of it. So year One made them both a bundle of nerves while trying to have sex. The next two years weren't much better.

In her junior year of college, Lance and Allison went their separate ways and after a short reflective break, she began dating Will. He was bright, an amazing cello player, volunteered to help the needy and was good at sports. All the things he hoped Medical Schools were looking for because his entire life was built around getting accepted into one. Anything he did brought up the question, "Do you think they'd like that?" If there was a competition as a poster boy for insecurity, Will was definitely in the running.

His insecurity crept into every waking moment of his life. Even when he and Allison had sex, every few seconds he could be heard asking for feedback. "It's good, isn't it?" "Are you liking it?" "Didja? Huh? Didja?" Will turned out to be a goalie protecting Allison from having an orgasm.

At the urging for friends, Allison finally sought out professional help. Her therapist said that she was now too uptight about sex. She had to learn to let go and see where things went. He suggested that a good way to do this was to take a vacation at a place like Club Med, particularly at an exotic location like Tahiti. Once there, she should find someone who she is attracted to and have wild sex with him. Then the therapist shocked Allison when he suggested that she not just surrender to sex with a stranger she was attracted to, but he should invite him to tie her up to underscore the idea of letting go.

When she left the therapist's office, she thought both he and the idea sounded crazy. But the more she thought about the kind of men she was currently dating and her longing for at least a hint of an orgasm, she went online and booked her reservation. It was a Club Med designed for single mid 20s to mid 30s. The next few weeks devolved into shopping sprees, looking at pictures of men in health magazines and giggling with girlfriends as they revealed wild sex stories they didn't usually divulge, but just this once because it was to help Allison. Her last act of shopping was a set of maroon velvet ropes.

The first night at Club Med featured a barbeque which was really a mixer where everyone could pick out a potential romantic object or three. Allison was almost giddy seeing how many men there were that would easily fit her loosely structured, watered down vacation criteria. The fact that Allison looked great in her bikini and a clear-cut above all the other women there didn't hurt her chances either.

As guys continued to buzz around her, she decided to do a quick study of Social Darwinism and see if the fittest survived. Garrett didn't just survive, he flourished. After five daiquiris and forty-five minutes of talking, they were back in Allison's hut. After a few minutes of making out, Allison surprised herself by still being able to blush as she handed Garrett her velvet ropes.

Garrett smiled and thought, "Great…a live one." There were a lot of things that Garrett had also always wanted to try and thought this was going to be his night. Before Allison knew what happened, Garrett was drawing up some complicated scenarios. He suggested first that they find another guy to have sex with Allison so that he could walk in and find them doing it. Then he would kick the other guy out, tie her up and then ...

Before he could even get to the part about how she got to discover that he had been wearing her underwear, she threw him out of her hut. The same hut that she refused to leave for the next three days. On the last night there, they had a farewell barbeque and she hooked up with David and felt some stirrings, but still no cigar.

Refusing Sex – If you try tying up a woman who refuses to have sex with you, find a brilliant defense attorney who is good at defending rape cases. It's going to be tough to tell the jury that the rope slipped out of your grasp and landed around her ankles and wrists and they got entwined around the bedpost.

A Case Study about Restraints (Refusing Sex)
Annette T. and John were just good friends. And they talked a lot about how they wanted to keep it that way. Annette loved the idea and John talked about loving the idea. Not surprisingly, he lusted after Annette in his heart and his loins, knowing that it was never to be. He made it a point not to even hug her for fear of giving himself away.

John was at home finishing a report for work when Annette called him up sobbing into her iphone. She had broken up with yet another guy lucky enough to sleep with her before breaking up. She asked if she could come over. She couldn't face being alone. What could a good friend say? Uh oh.

He was a bit surprised when Annette walked through the door. Her makeup was smeared and she was clutching a fairly large brown paper bag. She asked if he had any limes in the house. John said he didn't. Then she went into the kitchen and brought out a saltshaker. She sat down and took out a large bottle of tequila and asked him to bring two shot glasses. John tried to discourage her, but she was already opening the bottle.

Although he had to finish the report tonight, he took a few quick shots with her. Then a few more. Pretty soon, she was getting sloppy and falling all over John. He had been dreaming of a scenario like this, but was very wary. After a few more shots, he decided he could hold out no longer and made his move.

To John's surprise, Annette immediately suggested that they take it into the bedroom. Although Annette was finding it hard to talk, she managed to say, "If we're going to do what I think you think we're going to do, let's get a little crazy." She asked John to bring in some rope. She was going to tie him to the bed and assured him that he was going to go wild. John couldn't believe that his greatest fantasy was going to happen.

Annette quickly tied John to the bed, kissed him goodnight and thanked him for being such a good friend. She left and he did go crazy.

She Does But He Doesn't – The advantage of tying up a man who didn't when you did is that you can keep trying to get him to until he does. It helps if he has a good sense of humor.

A Case Study about Restraints (She Does But He Doesn't)

Brenda C. was getting worried. Her relationship with Eddie was hitting the five-month mark. It was getting close to the end of the "Infatuation Phase" of their relationship and she was aware of a very disturbing trend. Quite often in their lovemaking, she did, but he didn't.

Was he losing interest? Was there something wrong with her that her defenses wouldn't let her see? Was this another in a series of doomed relationships? She liked Eddie and didn't want to go down without a fight. There just had to be something she could do. She had gone through the usual channels to figure out what was wrong. She had spoken to her mother about it and she had consulted both Cosmo and Shape magazine. She came up empty. She was sinking into a mild panic episode.

But there was one source she hadn't tried yet. But did she have the nerve to go there? Carol was Brenda's best friend, her biggest competitor and by far the most sexually experienced of all her close circle of friends. It's hard to ask a competitor for help, even if she's also your best friend, but necessity makes strange bedfellows if you don't mind sleeping with a mixed metaphor.

As females go, Carol is way over on the belligerent side of the aggression continuum. She immediately pointed out to Brenda that Eddie was too secure in the relationship and wasn't feeling enough anxiety. He was way too dominant. When Brenda asked how she could make the bedroom more exciting for Eddie, Carol smirked and asked Brenda if she had four strong leather belts.

She suggested that the next time they went to the bedroom that she follow these three simple steps: (1) Get Eddie to drink a bit more than he usually does. (2) Tie his hands and ankles to the bed with the belts. When Brenda asked for the third step, Carol just smiled and said, "Honey, if your man is drunk and lashed to the bed and you have to ask for a third step, I can see why your relationship is in trouble."

That Friday night, Brenda put Carol's 2+ Step plan into action. Before she knew it, Eddie was drunk, tied and smiling. This got Brenda so hot that she jumped in and she did long before Eddie knew what was happening. But Brenda was now in no hurry and decided to go all out. She kept Eddie tied up while she put whipped cream all over him and licked it off. Then she started to spank him.

That night Eddie never did. But that just showed Brenda that he was the wrong guy for her. Now, every Wednesday night she and Carol go out cruising at a different leather bar and as far as Brenda is concerned, guys are responsible for their own orgasms and real men know that.

Small Breasts – Women with small breasts don't like to be tied up during sex. They tend to have an irrational fear that you're going to slip their bra back on and stuff it full of Kleenex. The more you protest that you would never do that the surer they become that you will. The best solution is not to wear a bra on your date. If he has his own bra... be even more wary.

A Case Study about Restraints (Small Breasts)

Sarah H. didn't like to go to gym glasses as a young girl. She didn't like to sweat and she didn't like to get dirty. She loved her Barbie's, helping mom in the kitchen and doing other girl things. She was a very feminine girl. As she continued to grow up, everything about her remained feminine except for two things... her breasts. They just didn't grow. She tried to eat more, do chest exercises and got hormone shots from the doctor. Nothing helped. She remembers the day in the 9th grade when everything changed. As the girls were changing for P.E. class, one of her friends was jamming her large breasts into her sports bra so she could get onto the field.

The words "Sports Bra" opened her life. She would dedicate her life to sports. When she wasn't participating, she wore warm up suits everywhere. Everyone would just assume she was wearing her sports bra. She didn't take public showers to hide her secret. Her life shifted 180°. She became an uber jockette. This left only one problem. She liked guys and they all thought she didn't like them.

It was assumed that Sarah was butch. To the other jocks, she was treated like one of the guys. This went on all the way through her final year of college. She was fed up with her life and wanted a man... in every sense of the word. Not knowing where to turn for advice, she decided to make an appointment at the University Counseling Center. She asked for a female therapist.

When she walked into the counseling office she became very self-conscious about being the only one wearing a tracksuit. The counselor was very supportive and listened very attentively to her story. She was very empathic and reflected that it must be very tough to keeping such a dark secret so close to the vest. The counselor had a very dark sense of humor.

Sarah said she didn't know where to turn. The therapist suggested that she try online dating so that she could separate her college social life from her problem. She also suggested that instead of giving an accurate picture of herself in her profile, she focus on the life she would like to have. She suggested that she not dwell on her athletic life so much.

As they talked, the therapist brought up a more sensitive issue. She pointed out that Sarah has ceded control of her life to everyone else's opinion of her. She needed to be in control. She should try to find someone she felt she could dominate. When Sarah asked how she knew she was in control and dominating, the counselor smiled and said, "Tie em' down on the bed. Literally be in control."

Sarah thought she found the right guy on the Internet and for the first few dates, she said they should move slowly and stay on first base. Kissing-yes...groping-no. Then after a few nights of this, Sarah was going to make the complete leap to full on sexual encounter. She prepared herself for the big night. They would drink a lot, the lights would be low, very low and he would agree to be tied up. Then they would finally have sex. It was a brilliant plan because with the lights dimmed and him being tied up, he would be so preoccupied that he wouldn't notice her lack of breastitude.

And it almost worked.

After he was tied up, she undressed and got on top of him, but she was not so good at knot tying. One of his hands got loose and he flailed as he reached for her breast. He reached several times and then got freaked out that he was tricked into bed by a man. By the time she turned on the lights, showed him her equipment and tried to get him to drink some more, he was putting on his clothes and running out the door.

Sarah decided that trickery was not the high-handed way to go through life. She was too honest and ethical. Her appointment with the surgeon for her implants is only two weeks away.

Overweight – If you are going to restrain an overweight woman, here are a few things to consider:

- Make sure you have enough rope, because if you don't she will be inconsolable.
- Have food within easy reach and give her some on request otherwise, she will think that the restraints are part of a new weight loss technique.
- Don't tickle her when restrained. You don't need a reason…just don't.

A Case Study about Restraints (Overweight)
Janelle R. couldn't spell the word "moderation." She studied hard, played hard and ate hard. Whatever she went after, she got. Quite often, that was a pizza. Although she was very intense, she was equally nice. Her friends were devoted to her and anyone who met her wanted to become her friend.

Janelle's problem was that she intimidated men. She was smarter than them, more successful than them and even stronger than them. This made for some lonely weekend nights while her other friends were off dating.

Her friends tried to explain to her that men tend to be really competitive and they like to win sometimes. She would have to learn to dial it down occasionally. Because of her size, she was particularly intimidating in bed. Men like to move women around during the act of lovemaking and Janelle was not movable unless she chose to move. That's when her friend Laurie came up with a great idea.

She suggested to Janelle that the next time she went to bed with someone, she asked that he tie her down on the bed. It would give the guy the illusion that he was the master of the bed. Janelle was game. Laurie set her up on a date and as a gift, got her two sets of handcuffs. Laurie knew that Jack, the guy she fixed Janelle up with was into some quirky stuff so Janelle would have a good shot here.

Jack was going through the motions of foreplay until Janelle brought out the handcuffs. He couldn't hide his delight. This was his turf. As Janelle tried to move around, the cuffs dug into her wrists and hurt her. She quickly understood that her job was to be submissive so she relinquished all control to Jack. That helped her wrists.

Janelle was shocked to learn how much pleasure there was in submitting. Before the night was over, she had already made another date with Jack. The next morning, she called Laurie who wanted to hear all the details. Janelle said she didn't have enough time for all that. She wanted to get the name of the shop that sold the handcuffs so she could order two more pairs for her ankles.

The Final Cure

Figure 1. People with no sexual problems

The end

www.ingramcontent.com/pod-product-compliance
Lightning Source LLC
LaVergne TN
LVHW020109100426
835512LV00041B/3235